# THE
# OUTRAGEOUS
# GRACE OF GOD

*Bill Little*

# THE
# OUTRAGEOUS
# GRACE OF GOD

TATE PUBLISHING
AND ENTERPRISES, LLC

Published by Tate Publishing & Enterprises, LLC
127 E. Trade Center Terrace | Mustang, Oklahoma 73064 USA
1.888.361.9473 | www.tatepublishing.com

Tate Publishing is committed to excellence in the publishing industry. The company reflects the philosophy established by the founders, based on Psalm 68:11,

*"The Lord gave the word and great was the company of those who published it."*

Book design copyright © 2015 by Tate Publishing, LLC. All rights reserved.
*Cover design by Joana Quilantang*
*Interior design by Manolito Bastasa*

Published in the United States of America

ISBN: 978-1-68237-522-8
Religion / Sermons / Christian
15.09.10

# ACKNOWLEDGEMENTS

I am grateful to the people who have helped in editing this material. They have offered helpful suggestions and given words of encouragement. These include Ed Viau, Barbara Davis, and Bill Carlin.

I would like also to acknowledge Dr. Sally Gafford who spoke strong words of encouragement during the time I was writing this material.

The Tate staff has been very helpful and gracious during the process of beginning and completing this publication. I thank them all.

# CONTENTS

# INTRODUCTION

THIS IS NOT breaking news. Our world is in a mess. We are in a mess. We have taken a lot of different roads to get here, but we are now here together.

It seems that all religions have gotten it all wrong. Religion should make the world a better, safer place to live, but too often the opposite is true. Fundamentalists from all major religions have focused on self-preservation and defense against those who disagree.

Such attitudes produce arrogant Pharisees. These are too often the religious leaders that cause some of us to cry out, "God save us from the 'good' people." These good people will hurt you if you are not a part of their group and if you don't agree with their creeds they are quick to condemn and very slow, if ever, to forgive.

Think about this: Religion should be inclusive but too often is exclusive. It should be accepting but too often is rejecting. It should be redeeming but too often is condemning. It should be loving but too often is filled with anger. It should be peaceful but too often is clamoring for war against those who don't agree with it.

What is a way out? I believe the way of grace is the way out. If we can embrace and accept the grace of God for ourselves and extend that to others we are on the right road. My prayer is that the material in this book will give us some direction and encouragement to believe it is not too late for us to find grace. I call it *outrageous grace* because it is so inexplicable and powerful. It is the good news. We are still in the circle of God's love and grace.

# DEFINITIONS AND EXAMPLES

I HAVE LONG struggled to get my mind wrapped around the meaning of *grace*. It is hard to understand the concept of getting something good that we don't deserve. I keep looking for examples of that concept. The first example that came to my mind was so mundane at first glance that I thought it was not a real example.

A friend had just finished medical school and was getting ready to move to Hawaii. He came by my house and handed me the keys to the old Ford that he had been driving while in school. He also handed me a signed title to the car and said, "This car is an old friend, and I want to give it to a friend. It now belongs to you."

The car was a very serviceable vehicle though about six years old at the time. I could use the car and I did. I didn't understand it at the time, but that was an expression of grace. I did nothing to earn or deserve the car, but it was given to me with no strings attached. My friend had shown me the meaning of grace, and I didn't understand that at the time.

On the other hand, I can contrast that experience with another one that was the opposite. I was having trouble keeping up with my second semester of Greek in college. Too many basketball trips and practices was my excuse. The Greek professor permitted me to take the final test late. I went to his home and sat at his dining room table to take the test.

When it was finished, I waited for him to grade the paper. I managed to barely pass the test, and with all my other course work, I was less than one point from making a C in the course. The professor told me that I would get a D for my semester grade. I was really disappointed.

I said, "I am only one point away from a C."

He replied, "You are one point short of a C and that is a D. I'm not Santa Claus."

Looking back on that experience I think I can grasp the difference between grace and law. The car was grace. The grade was legalistic and law. With those thoughts in the background, look at the following definition of grace.

Grace is undeserved spiritual gifts and right standing with God. We are saved by grace through faith and not by our works (Ephesians 2:8–9). That grace is more than amazing. It is outrageous. The fact that we are loved before we even believe in God is amazing. The fact that we can come to God and receive forgiveness for our sins is astonishing when you really think about it. We certainly don't deserve that grace and can do nothing to earn it. It does not end when we become believers. It goes on to cover not only our past sins but our future sins as well. It covers our sins and redeems us so that we are able to serve God no matter what has happened in our lives. Don't miss this point. No matter what you have been or done, if you accept the grace of God and ask for his forgiveness, you can serve Him right now.

Salvation is the free car. It is getting the grade that we do not deserve. We are getting an A. We don't deserve that A, but it is marked on our records. That is grace. Now, look at some real examples of spiritual grace that God gives to us:

- A shepherd boy was chosen to become the king of Israel. He was anointed by the prophet Samuel and did become king. He was said to be a man after God's own heart. After he became king, he was guilty of adultery and murder. Still, God used him to pen wonderful psalms and continue in the lineage of Jesus. That is outrageous grace.
- A disciple blatantly denied Jesus when His support was needed most. That disciple became one of the strongest leaders in the New Testament church. That is outrageous grace.

- A Franciscan priest, Brennan Manning, among other things, left the priesthood to get married. Sixteen years later was divorced. His divorce was at least in large part a result of his continued dependence on alcohol and regular alcoholic binges. He said of himself that he broke all the commandments. He said that he missed his mother's funeral because he stopped at a motel and drank himself into a blackout. Still, he was definitely in the circle of God's grace. During all that time, he led effective spiritual retreats and wrote some powerful spiritual material that continues to encourage and guide people to this day. That is outrageous grace.

- A thief and insurrectionist with only minutes to live was dying on a cross near Jesus. Jesus responded to his request to be remembered in His kingdom. Even though there was nothing this thief and convicted criminal could do for Jesus, He said, "Today you will be with me in paradise." That is outrageous grace.

- The apostle Paul confessed in Romans 6 that he struggled with failures in his own life. Note that he used the present tense when he spoke of doing what he knew was wrong and failing to do what he knew was right. He was admitting his imperfections even while he was being used to write the book of Romans. That is the outrageous grace of God in action.

When I read that again, I realized, "Wow, Paul's experience is a lot like mine." I discovered early on that sometimes the best and worst, good and bad, and the holy and profane lie down together in my mind and express themselves in my life. What a miserable man I am. Who can save me from all this? Thanks be to God, He can and will. That is outrageous grace for me. I will share my experience in greater detail later.

- In Luke 16, Jesus told a story we call the parable of the prodigal son. It is another illustration of the forgiveness and grace of God. The younger of two sons requested his inheritance from his father long before it was due. He then left home and squandered his inheritance on what is called riotous living. He found himself broke and scrounging meals from among the hogs. He decided that even his father's servants were better off, so he risked it and went home.

He had a speech prepared requesting a place among the servants, but before he said anything, his father saw him. He ran to meet the boy, threw his arms around him, and before the son said or did anything, the father had a feast prepared and welcomed him home. That is outrageous grace.

The elder son objected because he had stayed home and worked hard and had no feast. Too often churches behave like elder brothers and almost resent prodigals who come home. But where would prodigals go if there is no extreme grace of God available to them?

- In the John 8 there is a story of a woman caught in the act of adultery (the man must have gotten away). She was brought to Jesus by a group of religious people who pointed out that the law required her to be stoned to death. They asked him what should be done with her. After scribbling on the ground, Jesus stood and said, "Let the one who is without sin cast the first stone."

  One by one, her accusers sulked away. Finally, Jesus looked at the woman and said, "Is there anyone to condemn you?" She said, "No. there is no one." He said, "Neither do I condemn you. Go and sin no more." Oh, the outrageous grace of God!

- A somewhat similar story comes from more modern times. Jane was from a strong Christian family. She was popular among her peers, and many were sure she would be a missionary to some foreign land. She went away to college. There she started spending a lot of time with a gang of drug abusers. She became addicted to drugs and eventually became pregnant with one of the four or five young men she had sex with. Those who saw her during this time said she looked like death warmed over. Her family never gave up hope that she would return to her faith. After an abortion and months of struggle, she did return and a few years later, became a health care provider. She is today as lovely a Christian as you could ever hope to meet. Oh, the outrageous grace of God!

- Another young woman with a strong Christian background became pregnant and moved in with the father of the child. He claimed no faith background. She wanted to work with young people. Her goal was to help them not make the same mistakes she had made. Her pastor accepted her over the objection of a few members. She later married the young man she was living with and he became a Christian and both of them served independent missions in Africa. They and their children continue to serve in a local church. That is the outrageous grace of God.

This grace is such great news that one would expect to see a lot about it in the scriptures. That is, in fact, true. Here are a few examples:

- Nehemiah observed that even with repeated failures, God patiently preserved Israel. He said God was gracious and merciful.
- John 1:16–17 says that John the Baptist said of Jesus, "For of His fullness we have all received, and grace

upon grace. For the Law was given through Moses: grace and truth were realized through Jesus Christ."

- We are justified freely by God's grace (Romans 3:24).
- Paul reminds us that God's grace is sufficient for all that we ever need (2 Corinthians 12:9).
- In Ephesians 1, we read that we are lavished with the glorious grace of God.
- In Ephesians 2:8–9, we are told that we are saved by grace through faith. Paul begins all his letters with wishes for grace and peace. There is no permanent peace without grace.

# CONTRAST

BASED ON THE teachings of Jesus Christ and many examples as noted in chapter one, there are some wonderfully inspirational stories of forgiveness and grace. We all have heard stories of families that have forgiven acts of violence against them or their relatives.

One story that will remain with me all my life comes from an experience I had with a man whose beautiful teenaged daughter had been killed in an accident when a drunken driver ran into the side of the car she was riding.

After a couple of hours at a hospital where the girl had been pronounced dead, I went with him to another hospital for him to finish filling out necessary papers to make further arrangements. We rode the elevator there, and in the elevator this Christian man came over to me and said, "Pastor, let's pray for the man who hit the car and killed my daughter. He is going to have to live with this for the rest of his life." We prayed for that young man and for the comfort of both families affected by this tragedy.

That was an example of outrageous grace shared by one who was walking in the grace of God himself. There are many examples of that kind of grace.

But there is a tragic contrast between the grace described and practiced in the Bible and that practiced by too many in Christian churches. I recently attended a worship service in a church that is called by the name Grace. Signs were on the walls of the church reminding us of the wonderful grace of God. I then sat through a forty-five-minute message on the law. Again and again we seem to start with Jesus and wind up with Moses.

Jesus told a parable in Matthew 18 about the kingdom of Heaven. The king in the parable represents God, and the servants of the king represent all of us. One of the servants owed a huge amount to the king. He could not possibly pay it and begged the king to forgive the debt. The king graciously forgave the debt owed by the servant. That clearly represents the outrageous grace of God.

The servant found a fellow servant who owed him a small debt. Though the fellow servant begged to be forgiven, or at least given time to pay the debt, the servant who had been forgiven a huge debt refused to forgive his fellow servant. This clearly represents the lack of grace existing in the forgiven servant. God's grace is extravagant, but the servant's grace is miserly. The king rescinded the forgiveness he had extended to the heavily indebted servant. The message is simple: we who have been forgiven are to be free in our forgiveness of others. Miserly grace is a disgrace.

This is not a new problem. The entire book of Galatians was written by Paul to encourage the church to remain grounded in the gospel of grace and faith and not return to the law. Still, the problem persists.

Jesus consistently revealed the extreme grace of God, but in far too many instances the church that claims to be following Him has not exhibited much grace at all. Following is an example of the lack of grace one might find in such churches.

A young couple had been living together for several months and decided that they should get married. They went to the pastor of a protestant church and asked if he would perform their marriage ceremony. He said he could not marry them because they had been living together. Of course, he is the recipient of grace from God (undeserved), but he did not extend that same grace to that couple. That is an example of the miserly grace of the church in contrast to the outrageous grace of God. Even as I write this, I have to deal with the fact that I am not the judge of the minister involved, but I believe the act of rejecting the young couple is inconsistent with the grace of Jesus Christ.

The struggle continues for all of us who are involved in ministry of the church. We know the standards and we know that we fall short of those standards. We all therefore need the grace of God in our lives daily. We certainly want that, but we struggle with wanting to share that with others who obviously need that same grace.

We have seen television evangelists fall prey to their imperfections. Jimmy Swaggert was an example. He was able to continue his ministry after public attention was focused on his sexual failures. He found a measure of grace but was not able to continue with the same acceptance and support he had before the disclosure.

Popular preacher Jim Bakker also fell prey to the same problem. There was not much grace in the way he was rejected and treated even after he attempted to repent and ask for forgiveness. It did not appear that there were many who were willing to forgive him. We absorb grace better than we dispense it.

I know of a man who served as a denominational leader for at least fifteen years. He made a strong positive impact on church life in his denomination and was respected by others as an outstanding Christian leader. During the same fifteen years he was involved in a sexual affair that only ended after it was publicly exposed. Of course, he was then fired from his leadership position though he confessed and asked for forgiveness.

One friend said to me, "This is probably not an acceptable observation, but I wonder how he could do what he was doing while he was doing what he was doing. And I wonder if it could be possible for him to do any denominational work now." We both guessed not but wondered that he was able to do such an effective job for so long. I believe the answer must lie in the fantastic grace of God. God extends his grace but people do not. The same people who need grace—and we all do—deny it to others.

Situations like this are certainly troublesome because all us sinners want to maintain a higher standard than we are able to achieve, but we are afraid of becoming too permissive. It is a dilemma that has plagued the church since New Testament days. While holding up a higher standard of behavior we often lower the standard for showing grace and acceptance to the people who need it most.

I know we never fall beyond God's grace, but does that mean we can continue to serve him in meaningful ways? Manning seems to have done that. I guess the clearest answer to that question is grounded in the knowledge that all of us are sinners and none of us deserving of the opportunities we have. Remembering that fact and look at another example of one who was able to make significant contributions even while he failed morally then he lost it all.

The president of a national conservative Christian organization was exposed as having sexual failures in his life and was stripped of his role as a leader, and I have heard nothing about him in the years since. Apparently, he fell outside the church's circle of grace, and tragically, all the gifts God had given him will die with him. As inconsistent as it sounds, the Christian church is not known for permitting do-overs. At least we don't allow them for people who are known to have failed as long as we can keep our failures in the closets of our lives.

When we read of Stephen's execution by rock-throwing "good people" we see a clear contrast between the attitudes of deeply spiritual people and mean-spirited Pharisees. In Stephen, we see eyes of grace looking on a vicious mob and praying for God to forgive them. The mob, on the other hand, looks on Stephen with venom in their eyes.

One need not go back in history to see the violence and anger in mobs of self-righteous souls. Some claiming to be Christians cover their cowardly heads with sheets and participate in lynching men because they are different.

Hiding in groups, swastika-wearing gangs attack people of color and different race from their delusion that they are superior because of their skin color.

The greatest example of gracious attitude is seen in the crucified Jesus praying for His executioners: "Father, forgive them for they know not what they do." He then welcomed a crucified sinner to join Him in paradise just before He died.

The contrast is definite, but it is not always easy to tell the difference between the gentle spirited and the vicious ones until actions become clear. Jesus said that sometimes people appear to be lambs (gentle spirited) but are really wolves in sheep's clothing. You can only know them by their actions and attitudes. They may appear to be kindhearted and gentle in speech but underneath are unforgiving and judgmental people. It is hard to determine, but there is a contrast. One of the major differences is motive. Some people are more interested in destroying than in redeeming.

Certainly none of the failures from David down to present-day failures can be condoned and justified, but they all do not fall outside the circle of God's grace. They have none fallen so far that they could not be used in the kingdom of God if the church is open to them. These prodigals often have no home to which they can return. There are certainly no yellow ribbons tied to the doors of their churches or offices.

# WHY WE NEED GRACE
# REACHING FOR THE MOON

SINCE WE ALL fall short of perfection in our lives, we all need grace every day. It may be helpful for us to look at the reasons we need God's grace. Perhaps a few examples will clarify this need for us.

The clearest understanding of God's grace comes from an illustration by Max Lucado in his book *In the Grip of Grace*. Max suggests that we imagine that God tells us that in order to be forgiven and receive eternal life, we have to jump and touch the moon. We begin to jump and quickly learn that this is too much for us to ever achieve. Some of us jump higher than others, but none of us really come close. The only hope we have is that He will change the standard, and He has. He has jumped for us. He has freely given us forgiveness and eternal life if we are willing to accept it.

When I am told that I am to live by the teachings of the Sermon on the Mount (Matthew 5–7) I might as well have been told to jump to the moon. If the only way to eternal life is by living by these incredible standards, then my only hope is grace. I cannot come anywhere close to making that jump. That does not mean that I quit jumping. The Christian life is more about direction than it is about where we are.

William Barclay wrote in his *Commentary on the Book of Romans* that the Christian life means that we never disobey God. That life leads to what the scripture calls *sanctification*. He adds, "The word in Greek is *hagiasmos*. Greek nouns that end with *asmos* describe, not a completed state, but a process. Sanctification is not a completed state: It is the road to holiness." That leaves a little wiggle room but does not reach the heights yet. Because we have not yet arrived at a sanctified state, we still need grace.

We will never reach that completed state in this life because when one gives his or her life to Christ, that is not the end, and we do not become perfect. As William Barclay noted, "Christianity has always regarded the direction in which a man is facing as more important than the particular stage to which he has achieved."

Look again at the illustration of moon jumping. Strange things happen when we think we have to jump for the moon. Some who can jump as high as two or even three feet are judgmental of those who can only jump and inch or two. How ridiculous is that? Though none have come anywhere near the 230,000 miles necessary, some, in total arrogance, are audacious enough to judge others who haven't been able to jump as high as they have.

I thought that was a really good illustration until I began to read more about grace. Lucado mentions a very difficult point when he says he is bothered by the grace of God when it even reaches Jeffery Dahmer, the serial murderer who was guilty of ugly cannibalistic behavior. After imprisonment for his unspeakable crimes, Dahmer became a Christian while in prison. He was later murdered by an inmate but not before he had professed faith in Jesus and accepted forgiveness from God. We may be uncomfortable with that, but that is the outrageous grace of God.

I could easily look at Dahmer and say, "I at least jumped a couple of feet, but that guy hardly got his feet off the ground." It is hardly a recommendation for me that I can jump a little higher than Dahmer did. The fact is that none of us can reach high enough to not need grace.

We don't always recognize our need for God's grace, but it shows up anyway. I think of grace as a spiritual gift, but the fact is we live every day by God's grace. I had an experience a couple of years ago that brought home my own dependence on God's gift of life.

I was on my way to visit a patient when I had a sudden pain in my chest. The pain went down my left arm. I thought I knew what that meant. I pulled off on the shoulder of the highway and called my doctor, but he was not in. The pain went away.

I decided to go ahead and make the visit and drove on to the facility where the patient was. When I parked on the parking lot of that facility, the pain returned to my chest and arm. I sat in the car and decided not to go into the nursing home.

This was on December 17, the day of our hospice staff Christmas party. I made the decision to drive on to Maryville, Illinois, to the location of the Christmas party. It was a pleasant party. I had a good time and felt well until the end of the party. The pain did not return, but I began to feel weak.

There was no shortage of nurses. Three or four of them gathered around me and told me that I should go to the ER. Anderson hospital was less than three blocks away. After my wife's and nurses' insistence, I agreed to let our medical equipment manager drive me to the ER in his van.

I was examined and told that I should stay in the hospital. I again argued and said I could drive to Missouri and go the hospital where my doctor was on staff. The ER staff and my wife did not agree, and after more debate, I agreed to stay overnight.

At around one o'clock in the morning a nurse noticed a change in an enzyme in my blood, and I was taken to the ICU. I remembered very little after that. I do remember being very sick and being moved into an operating room. I did not know why.

The next morning I was told that my heart had stopped beating for a little more than three minutes. CPR and electrical shock restarted it. A stent was inserted into my heart, and I recovered quickly. Only had to stay one more night in the hospital and was back at work in one week.

The doctor told me that if I had had that heart attack any place other than the ICU, I would have stayed dead. I died for three minutes. That experience—getting sick three blocks from the ER, surrounded by nurses, taken to the hospital, and having a heart attack in the ICU—confirmed for me the relative insignificance of the material world and life in it.

Looking back, I just know that was all a gift from God. His grace gave me life to continue for a while and enabled me to continue seeing patients as their chaplain. I believe in the outrageous grace of God.

Still, I am plagued with enough pride that I decided to put together a balance sheet for myself. I put all the good things I have done on one side and the failures and misdeeds on the other. A lot more of my life was spent doing things that I deemed to be good things.

So I had preparing and preaching more than three thousand sermons, positive, helpful counseling time with hundreds of clients (many letters to prove it), seventeen years of responding to callers on CBS radio in St. Louis, cofounding the St. Louis Cancer Support Center, seeing more than a thousand patients and their families, having a dozen published books, visiting the sick, almost two years visiting hospice patients, spending hours in prayer and journaling, and the list went on, on the credit side.

On the debit side, I had personal failures with immoral behaviors, pride, self-aggrandizement, lying, and a few other shortcomings.

When I started evaluating all this and noted that there were thousands more things on the credit side than on the debit side, I shockingly realized that the sum of both was zero because only the righteousness of Christ fills our needs and His grace clears the table of sin. When applied to our spiritual needs, all our works amount to nothing, and we must rely on the grace of Jesus Christ alone. The failures amount to nothing when we accept the forgiveness and grace of Jesus Christ. We have nothing to really commend us to God, and nothing can condemn us when His grace covers us. That must seem outrageous to most people. I have no balance of good acts to commend me and, thank God, no balance of wrongdoings to condemn me. All is grace!

Not only is my spiritual salvation a gift of grace, my life is clearly a gift of grace. It always was; I just didn't realize it that clearly. Jesus said we could not add time to our own lives. I know that is true. I need God's grace for living, and I certainly need it for my spiritual well-being and so do you.

I cannot jump to the moon, live a perfect life, or add a day to my life. I thank God for His outrageous grace.

The bottom line is that we live in a mess, and grace is the only way out. Nothing else works.

In order to live a life that is in harmony with what is best in life and at peace with self, others, and God, we would have to overcome our failures, weaknesses, bad habits, and selfish behaviors. We would have to become free of our negative thoughts and bad attitudes. The struggle to do that is difficult and sometimes seems hopeless, but we continue to try. We can do a lot of helpful and good things, but none will be sufficient to lift us out of our failures and the problems we face.

We are mixtures of feelings, motivations, desires, and actions. I am one of those people. I find that I do things that I do not believe are right, and I tell myself I don't want to do them. What is wrong with me? Am I in touch with what I really want to do or not? I continue to wrestle with these questions every day.

Perhaps the answer is that I simply cannot be a consistent disciple of Jesus without totally relying on His grace. Manning says it best and clearly in his book *The Signature of Jesus*.

Manning's statement concerns real or radical discipleship. He says such discipleship "is pure grace to those who have no claim to it, for the deepest desires of our heart are not in our control. Were this not so, we simply would will those desires and be done with it." He then adds, "Without the grace of God, we cannot even desire God. Without the grace of God, I cannot walk the talk of Christ." Living in His grace is absolutely essential if we are to live for God.

# SOME THINGS WE TRY

THOUGH THE NEED for grace is clear, we have enough pride to think we can still do it ourselves. There are several interventions and concepts used to try to clear away the confusion and become more consistent in overcoming things we believe are not good for us. Here are some of the things that do not help solve our behavior and attitudinal problems. Barclay lists three of these things in his commentary on Romans 9.

We can do some good things that still fall short of the perfection we desire. Some try to find Utopia through learning more and more. *Knowledge* does not work. Addicts know that drugs are harmful and even deadly, but they use them anyway. Smokers know that tobacco smoke can lead to cancer and dozens of other diseases that are potentially deadly, still the knowledge does not stop them from smoking. Illicit sexual encounters are known to be risky, but that knowledge has done little or nothing to change sexual behaviors. Gambling can be addictive, and when that happens it can lead to bankruptcy, but habitual gamblers, knowing this, continue to gamble.

The scripture teaches that for one who knows to do right and fails to do that it is sin. This concept leads to the nagging fact that there are sins of omission. I am not only responsible for the wrong that I do but for the right things I fail to do. Still, I fail to do a lot of things that I know are right. Knowing brings responsibility but is not enough to correct our errors. It can help in some cases, but it does not solve our problems.

As a young man, I was aware of my lack of knowledge when it came to social graces. That often led to embarrassment for me. I didn't know how to hold a spoon. I didn't know how to ask to use the bathroom when I needed that knowledge. There was so much to learn, and I hoped that learning would save me from future embarrassment.

I discovered that there was too much to learn. At times I had to trust others to help me avoid problems. That lesson took me a long time to learn, and then I had to learn that all the knowledge in the world would not be enough. I would always need grace to bridge the gap between what I knew and what I needed to know. I have had an insatiable thirst for knowledge and am disappointed that the accumulation of it does not solve my problems in life. I wrote this verse that reflects my quest to learn more.

> Into the gourmet wines of life I plunge,
> With my soul the insatiable sponge.
> I soak up life until its pool is dry
> Then my searching eyes begin to cry.
> I drank beauty but I knew there was more to see.
> I drank knowledge but truth beyond will always be.
> I drank love and ached for one drink more,
> For all I drank left me thirsty as before.
> Satisfaction, to be totally and forever satisfied,
> Has eluded my soul no matter how I tried.
> Life said, "You can drink, drink all you will."
> So I drank and drank, but I'm thirsty still.

Having written that, I still know that knowing is simply not enough.

We try *resolutions*. Resolution does not work. We can resolve until we run out of paper on which to write resolutions and still have the problems we seek to avoid. Simon Peter is an example of this in the New Testament. He is reported to have said to Jesus in Matthew 26:35, "Even though I die with you, I will never deny you." You know how successful that resolution turned out to be. Every New Year's Day resolutions are made by the dozens, and seldom are kept beyond the first week of January. We resolve and then break the resolution. This just adds to our frustration in trying to overcome behaviors that we believe are not good for us.

*Diagnosis* does not work. We can know the diagnosis without ever finding the cure. I can diagnose myself as being one who eats too much and still gorge myself as often as I have a chance. I can diagnose myself as one who drinks too much and still drink to excess.

Many of my clients have asked, "Can you help me to understand why I do the things that I do?" I told them that I probably could but that knowing why would not change anything. We have to find more than understanding. We have to find ways to take action that produce changes in the behaviors that trouble us.

*Compromise* doesn't work. I know of people with a problem drinking who have said, "I can go into a bar with my friends and not drink. I'll just have a nonalcoholic beverage. I will not drink." They come out of the bar five hours later drunk as a skunk. I know others who have gambling problems who have said, "I can go into a casino and just watch people for a while, and if I gamble, I will limit myself to just a few dollars." They leave the casino hours later with no money in their pockets and a heavy charge card bill or large withdrawals from their ATMs.

I have known of men and women who have had trouble with sexual behaviors who kid themselves into believing that they can stop with just a hug or two, who wind up with unwanted pregnancies or venereal diseases. Compromise will not work.

Now, in reading Paul's comments to the Romans and with help from Barclay's commentary on that passage, I confirmed that knowledge could not solve that problem. I had plenty of knowledge about how gambling was ridiculous. It was bad for me. It was never going to be profitable for me. All that knowledge did not stop me from wanting to go back.

I know this is the same experience that cocaine addicts have. One professional athlete called me during spring training a few years ago and confessed that he had lied to me about using drugs. He said, "Bill, I have been using cocaine, and it is the hardest thing to quit that I have ever tried. The highs are so wonderful that I forget about the aftermath. I just want to experience it again and again." When any behavior is rewarded with a thrill that is quickly experienced after that behavior, it is terribly difficult to quit it. The thrill reinforces the behavior.

To help myself overcome my failures, I spent as much time as I could with people who seemed to be living victorious lives. We are certainly influenced by the company we keep, but I learned that it was not enough to just hang around with these people. It was good but not enough. I could live with a great artist and never learn to paint. I would have to learn fundamentals and practice for myself. That same principle applies to spending time with spiritual leaders. We need to learn from them and then practice what we learn.

Please do not misunderstand what I am saying. Knowledge can be and usually is a very good thing. Diagnosis is usually necessary before healing of addictions or disease takes place. Resolutions can help us make changes in our lives if we are diligent in pursing them. Compromise and accepting small approximations of our goals can be helpful if we do not stop there. Spending time with people who are really seeking to live for God is a good thing. I am saying that while these are often necessary in life, they are not sufficient to overcome our failures and become what we are created to be.

We have to change our focus and our framework for living. It is necessary to move from self-seeking to seeking what is in the best interest of all. When I believe in something that I am willing to live for and even to die for, I will be motivated to seek the best ways to achieve that. Honestly, there are few things that grab me that clearly, so how can I improve my living? The answer is to accept the outrageous grace of God by faith. I believe in God's grace expressed in Jesus Christ, and I accept it as a free gift from Him.

# NOT EVERYONE LIKES GOD'S GRACE (FOR OTHERS)

MOST OF US would agree that God's grace is available to all and especially us average sinners or even some of us pretty blatant sinners but people like Jeffery Dahmers? I like it when God's grace covers my sin, but I am not always sure about his or yours. Does God's grace cover the really bad sin? What a question! Isn't all sin really bad? Isn't all sin covered by the same grace of God? Is it true that none of us ever fall beyond the reach of that grace and God's love?

That question is raised by Brennen Manning in his book *It's All Grace* when he asks how far the grace of God reaches. He partially answers this question when he refers to the thief on the cross who made a request to Jesus from his deathbed, or his death cross. The answer is disturbing to many. Yes, not only can it reach that far but it has. As mentioned above, in the last moments of his life on the cross, Jesus extended grace to this dying thief.

At first glance, that kind of grace seems to be impossible or at least too good to be true, but I thank God that it is true. I can't reach the moon, but I can accept the gift of God's grace to forgive me and redeem me no matter what has happened in my life, no matter how often I have failed and fallen. That is the good news of the gospel.

Of course, many are disturbed by the experiences of Brennen Manning and experiences of others like him. But I have read materials written by Manning. He wrote some wonderful material about spiritual growth. He was a popular speaker for spiritual retreats and religious meetings. He clearly seems to have been loved and revered by people who read his works, heard him speak, and been in groups with him.

Manning's books made a strong impression on me because I have long had a problem with organized religion of all kinds and certainly with the Christian religion. I was encouraged and heartened by what I read in Manning's books. Following are some illustrations that are important for me.

Manning served the Little Brothers of Jesus by doing menial tasks to help people in the villages around them. He said, "One of my realizations in such an earth atmosphere was that many of the burning theological issues in the church were neither burning nor theological. It was not more rhetoric that Jesus demanded but personal renewal, fidelity to the gospel, and creative conduct."

He later quotes the Episcopal priest Robert Farrar Capon who wrote about vulgar grace:

> "In Jesus, God put up a gone fishing sign on the religion shop. He has done the whole job in Jesus and simply invited us to believe it—to trust the bizarre, unprovable proposition that in him, every last person on earth is already home free without a single religious exertion: no fasting until your knees fold, no prayers you have to get right or else, no standing on your head with right thumb in your left ear and reciting the right creed—no nothing... The entire show has been set to rights in the Mystery of Christ—even though nobody can see a single improvement. Yes, it is crazy. And yes, it is wild, and outrageous and vulgar. And any God who would do such a thing is a God who has no taste. And worst of all it doesn't sell worth beans. But it is Good News—the only permanently good news there is—and therefore I find it absolutely captivating." (*All is Grace*, 193)

With all the problems, he was a remarkable man, and I love reading his material. He could have been spiritually sensitive and insightful only through the amazing grace of God. I know people who do not like to accept the fact that God's grace was sufficient for his life's situation.

The parable of Jesus (Matthew 20:1–16) about the workers who are hired early in the morning, others a few hours later and others the last hour of the day, sheds light on the extent of grace. When the owner of the vineyard came to pay the workers, he gave everyone of the same wage. The early hires complained but were told that they were given exactly what they agreed to receive. I can understand their concern. They didn't want equal treatment for those who had not done as much as they had. The grace of God is like that. It is extended to anyone who accepts it at any hour of the day or time in life. I have no room to complain if I have received grace for myself. What you receive is between you and God, but some people do not like that system.

The elder brother in the parable of the prodigal son (Luke 14:11–31) is another example of people who not only don't like the reach of God's grace but actually resent it for people they think less deserving than they.

Ideally, the moment the elder brother heard that his kid brother had returned home, he would have run to greet him and tell him how much he had been missed. That probably would never have happened no matter how the father received the prodigal. Grace is a wonderful thing for us, but when it is extended to some undeserving and irresponsible young ingrate, that tends to gall us. Notice, I said *undeserving*, but aren't we all?

It may be hard to grasp but the grace of God is freely given to all, regardless of what they have been or done. That should be seen as good news because none of us deserves that grace. It sounds like good news to me. If any readers of this material have become discouraged with failures in your own lives, take heart. You have not fallen beyond God's love, and you can still be a servant in His kingdom's work.

# HOW MUCH SIN IS TOO MUCH
## FOR GOD'S GRACE?

YEARS AGO I heard a story attributed to the owner of the Washington Redskins football team. He is reported to have told this concerning former great NFL coach George Allen. He said that he gave George an unlimited budget to help build their football team and George overspent it. We have received an unlimited budget of God's grace. It is doubtful that it is possible to overspend it.

The examples of sinful people who were permitted to effectively serve God raise questions for many, if not most people. To answer some of those questions, I return to Lacado. One of the best illustrations of the extent of grace I have ever seen was in Max Lacado's book *In the Grip of Grace*. He tells a humorous story about having his insurance cancelled. He says the company informed him that he had exceeded his limit in accidents. He said, "I thought the reason I had the policy was because I might have accidents." He said he didn't know he would be limited and they would cancel his policy when he maxed out (pun intended) on accidents.

God apparently does not have a limit on our sins. No matter how much we had sinned before accepting His grace and no matter how much we sin after accepting that grace, it is sufficient. We are no more or less deserving of God's grace now than when we first accepted it.

A man prayed, "God, I have sinned again and am no longer worthy of your grace and forgiveness." It is probable that God said to him, "Who said you were worthy when you first received my grace?" We are never worthy. That is why it is called grace.

We do not have to worry about God cancelling our policy because we have had too many failures. We cannot overspend our budget. This is not to minimize our failures but to maximize the extent of God's amazing and outrageous grace. It is also meant to give hope to people who know they have failed and who are miserable in that knowledge. Some live in hopeless despair because they see no hope for ever meaningfully serving God again. Please note this. There is a place for you in the service of God.

I heard of a life insurance policy that requires no physical examination and can never be canceled for any reason. I don't have that policy, but it sounds like something I'd be comfortable owning.

I have a grace policy that did not require an examination, and it can never be canceled. According to Romans 8 there is therefore no condemnation to those who are in Christ Jesus. And that chapter closes with the promise that nothing, absolutely nothing, can separate us from God's love. Even prodigals are still loved by the father.

It is true that elder brothers don't always welcome prodigal brothers home. Church people don't always welcome sinners. Pharisees are still a major problem for religion. It is true that people who began working early in the morning are angered when people who started much later in the day receive the same pay they are getting. When that happens, people are forgetting that none of us deserves the good that we are receiving. Pharisees are still thanking God that they are not like these tax collectors and sinners. And sinners still beat their chests asking for mercy (Luke 18:9–14).

The good news is that God never stops giving mercy to those who ask for it. That message is considered by some to be dangerous. It seems to give too much liberty to sinners. But the question is not is this a dangerous message, but is this a true message? I believe it is true.

Grace means that nothing we do can ever separate us from God's love for us and eternal life. Some object that this is a risky thing to teach and preach. It certainly is.

Charles Swindoll agrees that it certainly is risky and there are constant temptations to abuse it. He makes a dramatic claim quoting Martyn Lloyd Jones who said that grace was not only risky but also downright dangerous. Meaning what? People will misunderstand real preaching on grace. Some people will misrepresent grace and take advantage of it. That is going to happen.

Swindoll adds, "To all my fellow ministers I must add my voice to that of Martyn Lloyd Jones: If you claim to be a messenger of grace, if you are really preaching grace, yet no one is taking advantage of it, maybe you are not preaching it hard enough or strong enough." He says that grace-killing, legalistic preachers will never be misunderstood in that way. He then clearly adds that preaching grace may indeed be risky, but it is worth the risk.

We are justified by grace through faith. Again, I quote Swindoll from his book *Grace Awakening*: "Justification really means this: Even though I still sin periodically and have found myself unable to stop sinning on a permanent basis, God declared me righteous when I believed. And because I will continue to sin from time to time, I find all the more reason to be grateful for grace. As a sinner I deserve vengeance. As a sinner I am afraid of justice. And so, as a sinner, my only hope for survival is grace. In its purest form, it makes no earthly sense." God's grace is absolutely outrageous for all of us, and I love it!

# GRACE DOES NOT CONDONE
# NOR EXCUSE SIN

THE APOSTLE PAUL makes it crystal clear in Romans 6:13–18 that free grace is not an excuse to sin nor does it mean that sin is condoned. It has consequences, but those consequences are not expressed in terms of rejection. Some who commit murder can be forgiven but still have to serve time in prison. Even a traffic violation usually means at least a fine. But spiritually, we are lifted above consequences by the grace of God when we are willing to accept it, and we are declared to be righteous.

Certainly, this is a dangerous doctrine. There will be people who misunderstand it and abuse it, but it is still true and is the source of our liberty (freedom) to be who we are and do the best we can.

I love basketball and played for as long as I could. My goal was to make every shot that I took and to stop my opponent from scoring at all. Those were my goals. I never achieved them, but I never excused myself for failing. I would go back to the gym and practice more and more. I developed into a very good shooter but never was perfect. Still, I regretted every missed shot.

My goal as a Christian is to be like Jesus Christ and obey his commands. I have not achieved that goal, but I keep going back to practice and study more to keep moving in that direction. It is a direction of hope. Robert Louis Stevenson said, "To travel hopefully is better than to arrive." I don't know about that because I have not yet arrived, but I travel on with hope. I still regret every missed shot and know that I am ultimately dependent on God's outrageous grace.

I never condoned a missed shot in basketball, and I never condoned sin in my life. I practiced more and more shots that I had missed. I studied, prayed, and sought help with the sins that most often beset me. They were like thorns in my flesh. Because of my nature as a human being I cannot not sin, still I will keep trying to overcome sin and seek God's grace to cover them, not condone them.

King David certainly was guilty of sin, and he received grace forgiving him of that sin, but that did not stop the consequences. Read Psalm 51 where David pleaded for God to create in him a clean heart. His sin was constantly in his mind, and he wept over it.

Most of us deeply regret our sins, and we do not excuse ourselves. We just ask for grace and keep moving forward.

It seems to me that the church is on that same journey I am on. None of us have reached the destination, but we are not in the role of judge and punisher for sinners. The church is to be in a redemptive role for all—even the prodigals. If the church turns its back on the sinners, where are they to go? Maybe we can get going together in the right direction.

It is also true that we are expected to forgive and extend grace to others just as we have received grace ourselves. Read Luke 18. With all that God has forgiven us, wouldn't it be outrageous for us not to forgive others when they sin against us?

When I referenced this command on forgiveness in my book, *The First Stone*, one man said to me, "I can't forgive sin. Only God can forgive sin." I responded by telling him that only God can ultimately forgive our sins, but many times he told the disciples and—through them—all of us to be forgiving of one another. It is part of the Lord's Prayer. It is certainly a consistent teaching of Jesus.

In Matthew 18:21–22, Peter asked Jesus, "How often must I forgive my brother? Shall I forgive seven times?"

And He answered, "Not seven times but seven times seventy."

God forgives not excuses.

We should not be surprised that a good many people will interpret these comments about grace as another excuse for their sin. This is not the purpose of grace. We all like to find excuses for our misbehavior. It is common to hear the expression "It's not my fault."

Charlie Sykes wrote a book a few years ago titled *Nation of Victims*. In it he says that we have developed a nation of victims because we find excuses for just about everything. He suggests that many psychiatrists, psychologists, and social workers are the culprits.

One example he gave was of a teacher who continuously showed up for work late in the mornings. She was warned several times and then put on probation. She continued to show up late. She was fired.

She hired two people. She hired a psychiatrist and a lawyer. The psychiatrist diagnosed her as having a chronic lateness syndrome. I never heard of it but probably it could be called something like CLS. While reading this, I thought that is a condition that could be cured with an alarm clock.

This is not to suggest that there are not people who have legitimate conditions that interfere with their daily functioning. It is to suggest that we have probably gone overboard on excusing bad behaviors by simply categorizing them as some illness or condition.

The lawyer who took her case won, and she had to be reinstated. It simply wasn't her fault.

He gave another example of an unusual sickness. An FBI agent stole money from his office and used it to gamble. He lost. He also was caught. He hired two people, a psychiatrist and a lawyer. The psychiatrist diagnosed him as having a compulsion to gamble with other people's money. He was reinstated but probably confined to office duties.

The point is that it is too easy to blame everything on some mental problem, a dysfunctional family, poor training, or some other problem. At some point many of us just have to accept responsibility for our actions, confess them, and ask for God's grace to forgive us.

No matter what you do you can more than likely find someone who will give you psychological absolution or help you find some other excuse for your behavior. Just remember to seek a healthy balance between real problems and excuses. God forgives in His wonderful and outrageous grace, but He does not condone.

Not only are we not excused from sins of commission, we are not excused from sins of omission either. We are expected to do good when we know to do it. The standard for living a Christian life is as high as the moon. We are to strive to live it daily. If you have received God's grace in your life, you probably are motivated to do as much good as you possibly can and still rely on God's grace to bridge the gap between what you are and what you should be. That is what grace is about.

# HOW GRACE CAN AFFECT OUR JUDGMENTAL ATTITUDES AND FORGIVENESS

KNOWING THAT WE need grace every day and that we are all guilty (Romans 3:9) should be enough to stop us from judging one another. Paul makes that very clear in Romans 2.

The first time I recall reading that passage it fell on me like a ton of bricks. I was visiting with friends after a church service. I was an arrogant young preacher in contrast to an arrogant old one. We had just come from a service where we listened to what I would call an eternal sermon. It seemed to have no place to end. The preacher obviously had no preconceived outline and was just freewheeling from one passage of scripture to another. This went on for well over an hour and a half.

I decided to really drive home the point about his style. I said to my friends, "I think he just opens the Bible and points to a passage and starts there. Maybe like this." I opened a Bible from an end table and randomly pointed to this passage in Romans 2. I started reading as if I was going to preach from the passage and I read, "Who are you to judge another when you are guilty of the same thing." Two of my friends and I were embarrassed and decided that we had just unfairly judged another.

We are all guilty of the same things: sin, failure, imperfection, and violation of the guidelines set forth by Jesus Christ. We may not all commit the same errors, but we all commit errors (the same thing). None of us have any right to judge others of us.

In Matthew 7:1–5, judging is not a part of the Christian's job description. Jesus forbids judging and gives two reasons. He warns that judgmental people will be judged with the same measure with which they have judged others. He then says that those who judge are frequently guilty of worse things than the person they are condemning. He asks, "How can you see to judge the tiny speck in another's eye when you have a log in your own eye? Take care of your own problems then you may not be so anxious to judge someone else."

Our first order of business is to look at our own flaws. I like the old saying "There is so much good in the worst of us and so much bad in the best of us that it hardly behooves any of us to talk about the rest of us." There is so much bad in me that I can ill afford to be judgmental of others.

As in all the laws given for guidelines in the kingdom of God, this one too is very practical. We are not equipped to judge others because we simply do not know enough about them. I have enough trouble judging whether I am living in or out of the kingdom of God. I certainly cannot judge how well others are living in or out. Doing so would certainly put me out.

Several years ago, I came upon a car that appeared to be stalled on the off-ramp of a highway. I decided to use my relatively new car and risk giving the man a push. He was standing outside his car and certainly appeared to need help. I began to move toward his car. I lowered my window and asked him to see if the bumpers matched (that was a long time ago when bumpers were still in use). He began frantically waving his arms and yelling at me to get away from his car.

I thought to myself that he must be some kind of ingrate. I was irritated but backed away and drove around his car. When I passed by, I saw that a jack was supporting the left front bumper of the car and the left front wheel was off. If I had even slightly bumped the car, the left side would have been grounded.

I did not have enough information to judge him as an ingrate and become irritated with him. I needed to survey the whole situation before making any kind of evaluation. In most cases, we do not have enough information about others to make judgments about them. Another practical reason for not judging others is that none of us is completely impartial. I certainly would judge my son or daughter with more leniencies than I would the son or daughter of someone I do not know.

It is much easier to embrace the non-judgmental attitude when we accept the guidelines of the Sermon on the Mount than when we embrace the legalism of Sinai. When I have a set of laws to govern what is right and what is wrong, I can easily apply them to you. If you don't measure up to my system, you are judged to be a guilty lawbreaker. The instructions to be merciful make it less acceptable to judge others or ourselves for that matter. Grace is a roadblock to judgmental attitudes.

It is easier to judge when we generalize—all whites, all blacks, all Christians, all Muslims, all of anything is a prelude to judgmental attitudes. When I meet people and get to know them one-on-one, I am not nearly so likely to be judgmental. When we adopt the motto from Stephen Covey's book *The 7 Habits of Highly Effective People*, "Seek first to understand and then to be understood," it will change our outlook dramatically. Once I begin to understand you, I am probably going to learn that we have a lot in common, and you become easier for me to accept. When we reverence and respect others as of equal value to us, we may be better able to extend grace to them.

Wouldn't it be wonderful if everyone could really understand you? If they knew what all you have been through and how you got to be who you are now, they would certainly find it easier to appreciate you. But getting to know you would require a lot of effort. It is less stressful to simply judge you by the surface that I see. Judging is a lazy way of dealing with people.

When I was in seminary, I heard a remarkable story about judging. It seems that there was a conductor on a train who was having trouble remembering his responsibilities. He forgot to return to some passengers who had asked for information about the schedule for the next stop. The passengers began to complain first to one another then directly to the conductor.

The conductor apologized then absentmindedly walked on through the train. A second conductor came through the car and heard the men complaining. He explained that the first conductor had found out at the last stop that his wife had just died. He was told that he could just ride the train on home but that he thought continuing to work would help him keep his mind off his grief.

Once the explanation was given, the attitudes of the formerly irate passengers changed by 180 degrees. Often there are reasonable explanations for behaviors in others. When we learn to stop judging and begin understanding, we will feel better about others and ourselves.

I learned years ago that it could be helpful whenever I hear someone harshly speaking of someone if I can honestly say, "That's interesting. I heard him say how much he likes you." If I don't have that information, I can say, "I wonder what he thinks of us?" Statements or questions like these can be what some call pattern breakers. They cause people to stop and think about what they are saying. It is amazing how often we speak without giving thought to the content and consequences of what we are saying. Practicing these pattern breakers will enable us to extend grace to others.

Years ago a young woman began visiting the services at the church I served as pastor. She wore jeans and dirty sneakers before it was cool to do so. She would come in to a service, sit near the front of the sanctuary, and swing her feet over the back of the pew in front of her.

That same scenario took place repeatedly for several months. Eventually, she became a member of the church.

After her family had moved out of our area about ten years later, I received a letter from her. She informed me that when she visited our church, she was about finished with church and decided to try us out. She deliberately behaved in a way that she thought would mean she would be rejected. She was not.

She was a prodigal looking for acceptance. Thank God, she found it. I have wondered often since that episode, have we provided an atmosphere where prodigals feel welcome or are we too judgmental? I am certain that we are often guilty of creating judgmental environments.

Have you ever been misjudged by someone? If so, how did you feel? That has happened to me on more than one occasion. Remembering that, I ask if I have ever misjudged anyone. The answer is certainly yes. How about you?

There are good reasons for obeying this command of Jesus, but the primary one is that it is His command. He is our God, and we are to obey Him.

The fact is that since we are all saved by grace, living by grace, forgiven by grace, how could we get the idea that we have a right to judge anyone? Perhaps the most apparent reason for not judging others is that we are all guilty of the same things and in equal need of God's grace. The first chapter of Romans makes that point very clear.

# LEGALISM AND MORALITY

IF YOU SPEAK out for liberty and grace and in opposition to legalism, you might be a grace preacher. I hesitated to include this topic. Some of the issues in this chapter will seem so petty that many people will not believe they are serious issues with which we should deal. I hesitated and then reread Charles Swindoll's book *The Grace Awakening* and then on further reflection decided that this may be one of the most significant challenges that Christians face. It can become a problem for anyone who is influenced by legalism and the harsh judgmental attitudes it spawns.

*Legalism* (in religion) is an attitude and mind-set that seeks to control others through authoritative laws and rules. The laws are usually said to come from God or to at least be inspired by God. The idea is to intimidate people who may disagree.

Legalistic religion is not just dangerous. It is evil. It accuses grace teachers and preachers of being antinomian (against the law). We are not against the law; we just want to be clear on the *role* of the law. It has no power to save people. It is a tool for separating right from wrong. With no law, there would be no sin. But showing us the law does not forgive our sins or save us from them; only grace can do that. Legalistic religion is antigrace. Swindoll says it is a "grace killer." It robs us of liberty and joy in our faith.

Legalism was certainly present in early Jewish religion. It was not enough to have the Ten Commandments. The religious leaders needed more specific laws to govern and control the people, so they added more and more laws to control daily lives. The laws were so numerous that it took rabbinical groups to interpret and teach them. Religion was certainly not a subject that was understood by the common people, and the religious leaders wanted to keep it that way.

Early Christianity experienced the same problem. People who became Christians by grace were led to revert to outward observance of the law in order to continue in the Christian life. The entire book of Galatians is devoted to correcting that false teaching. Much of the book of Romans deals with the subject as well.

First there were the leaders who wanted the early Christians (the gentiles) to submit to the Jewish rite of circumcision. Paul confronted and rejected that proposal when he wrote the book of Galatians. He then also had to confront the legalistic position that Christians could not eat meat offered to idols.

The controversy arose because of the practice some had of making meat offerings to idols. Not the whole body of meat was offered to the idols, so butchers got the remains and sold them in their shops. The meat was not harmed. Idols of wood or stone certainly had no power to contaminate the meat. Still, there were those who said that Christians should not eat it. Paul pointed out that that was not only erroneous but *any addition* to the message of salvation by grace through faith was in error. He told the Christians to simply give thanks and eat the meat.

The issues in modern days are just as distressing as the legalism of the early church. We have replaced grace with legalism. The legalists say, "If you do this, you are not being a Christian." That statement is followed by any one of a list of things considered sinful. We cannot discard grace. The bottom line is that you cannot begin with Jesus (grace) and then end with Moses (law). Start in grace, continue in grace, and end with grace. Grace brings liberty into our lives and enables us to be more than we have ever been before.

Early in my Christian experience I was urged not to major on the minors. Over the years, I have struggled to differentiate between the majors and the minors, and that is not always an easy task. Some will find it difficult to believe, but I grew up in churches where dancing and social drinking were seen as major moral problems. I want to speak to these issues and a few others. Before dealing with a few specifics, I note that the whole area of evaluating morality requires a kind of judging that can become blind and cruel.

No situation ever made clearer the reasons for the admonitions of Jesus when He commanded us not to judge in Matthew 7. The command was not a command to ignore immoral behavior but a practical command to avoid judging others. The reasons were presented as follows: First, when we judge others, we fail to see our own sins and failures. It is the eye problem of specks and two-by-fours. When we judge others, we are blinded by a two-by-four in our own eyes. Blind guides are awful, but blind oculists are beyond comprehension.

The second reason for not judging is that when we judge, we lose sight of not only our own failures but the good in the other person.

The third reason for not judging is that we bring the same kind of judgment that we render on others down on ourselves. The fallout from those judgments remains to be seen.

The final reason for not judging is that it is simply outside our job description. That is God's area. Some do a better job of remembering that than the extreme conservatives. We all need second chances, and some of us even need third and fourth chances. What we need is mercy, but we do not receive it unless we give it. Jesus said in Matthew 5 that the merciful will receive mercy.

Some general examples will help to clarify the impact of legalism on moral attitudes. Don't stop reading when you see the topics. As hard as it is for some to believe, these are actual issues among many Christian groups. It will take courageous prophets to confront these minor problems. They become major when they are coupled with legalistic mind-sets.

## Movies

Legalists have rules against a lot of things. There are still church groups that categorically condemn all movies as sinful. You might smile at that notion, but it is no laughing matter. It has become far less of a problem with the widespread presence of television. Movies have become a part of our daily culture, so even the most legalistic people have backed off on their insistence that this form of entertainment is an evil to be avoided by Christians. This is not a defense of blatantly violent and sexually explicit programs. It is a defense of the right to choose.

## Dancing

This is another issue that will surprise people outside ultraconservative religious groups. The legalism that thoughtlessly stands against dancing leads to hypocrisy. I have known people who publicly opposed dancing but privately subscribed to pornography. Go figure!

Years ago, the association of churches of which I was a member, kicked out a church that sponsored a square dance in their basement. That same association for years defended the separate but equal approach to education and worship. Most of the churches in that association were promoting segregation. Not one church was ever excluded for racism. There were rules against dancing but none against racism. Is that a focus on majors or minors? Is that not a topic for grace preachers and teachers to challenge?

The argument against dancing is that dancing can stimulate sexual feelings. Some adults have forgotten that when you are between the ages of sixteen and twenty-five (or sixty), a sneeze can be sexually stimulating. I am saying that if you are going to forbid every behavior that can be sexually stimulating, you are going to have to insist that everyone just sit perfectly still.

What has all this to do with the impact of legalism on morality? Morally, I find no fault with social dancing. I would never storm the school board meetings to protest a high school–sponsored dance for the senior class. Legalistic fundamentalists did just that in the southern part of the state where I live. I never understood their reasoning or lack thereof. Would you rather have young people attending a school-sponsored dance or going on a date and sitting in a parked car for two hours? Where is the spirituality in that?

## Social Drinking

Legalists have rules. No alcohol is the rule. The first time I was with a minister who ordered a cocktail, I inwardly cringed. I later found that man to be one of the finest Christians I have ever known. He remains one of my closest friends to this day. I am thankful that my initial reaction was not verbalized. I am sure there were others who thought I was associating with a "wine bibber." I was not. He drank gin. My reading of the scripture leads me to the conclusion that it is drunkenness and not social drinking that is a problem to be avoided.

Since that time, I have felt free to be with people who were having a cold beer to relax on a hot summer day. I am free to join them, but I have never developed a taste for alcohol.

I would not hesitate to join Jesus in a glass of wine (perhaps that He had made) at a meal. I know the argument that I should do nothing that would cause my brother to stumble. To take a teaching that was directly related to eating meat that had been offered to idols and make a cross-cultural general application of it seems to be a stretch. Paul spoke to that issue in the book of Galatians, a required reading for legal moralists.

We have precious little time to spend in preaching and teaching. It is immoral to misuse that time by focusing on things that do not really make much difference. I become frustrated with obese ministers preaching on the evils of a social drink. There is much more freedom to have a social drink based on the scriptures than there is justification for gluttony. To me, the obese minister is straining at a minor (gnat) and swallowing a lot of majors (camels or beef).

I took a guest with me to a very conservative church service. Of all mornings, that morning, the minister used an example about the dangers of social drinking. He said that he would not even drink orange juice from a glass that looked like a liquor glass. At least he wouldn't do that in front of a window where someone might see him and think that he was having a drink of alcohol. That is an example of legalistic hogwash.

After the service the guest said to me, "Was he serious about not drinking juice from a glass that looked like a liquor glass?"

I said that I was sure that he was.

The response was, "That is crazy. What is wrong with a social drink anyway?"

"Darned if I know."

I was thinking about the admonition of Paul for Timothy to drink a little wine for his stomach's sake. I was thinking about Jesus making wine—not just wine, but the best wine—for the wedding in Cana. I was remembering visiting a dinner with one of the finest Christian men I have known. It was a dinner with a priest and four nuns. They offered a glass of sherry after dinner. My friend saw my discomfort. It was several years ago, and my strict background was generating some anxiety. He spoke quietly to me, "This is an expression of their hospitality. The least we can do is sip it with them."

I did, and nothing awful happened to me. I am not a social drinker simply because I do not enjoy the taste of most alcohol. But I find no fault with drinking in moderation. I even believe that eating should be done in moderation!

## Divorce

A major question with which many of us have long grappled is divorce. I know of no one who thinks divorce is generally a good thing, but it seems to me that we have not dealt fairly or adequately with this question. I will write more later about my experience with divorce, but a comment here seems appropriate in relationship to legalism.

The strict legalist gives no room for divorce except in some cases of adultery. That is a position that takes the words of Jesus on this issue from the Sermon on the Mount and holds it literally. (It is interesting to note that these same people who often take other statements from the Sermon on the Mount far less literally.) Failure to turn the other cheek when suffering physical attack is understandable. Maybe the same reasoning applies to divorce.

I have long believed that legalistically forbidding divorced people to serve in positions of church leadership is wrong. I reasoned that we accepted people who had been convicted of crimes, people who had repeatedly committed adultery, and people who were openly prejudiced against certain minorities, as well as those who may have told a few lies. Then why would we single out divorced people for rejection? Doesn't grace and forgiveness come into play for all us sinners?

It seems to me that there are many situations where divorce is the lesser of evils. The most dramatic one is in the case of spousal abuse. No person should be expected to remain in an abusive relationship.

This was my position for thirty years before I experienced divorce myself. I had more trouble accepting my own situation than I did that of others, but the church I had served for more than forty years asked me to continue as their pastor. In fact, they exhibited a fantastically supportive attitude and helped me through the experience. I cannot imagine that happening in an extremely legalistic church.

The problem is one of consistency in dealing with all human failure. There is no question but that we must draw lines in what is acceptable and what is not. At the same time, we must honestly ask ourselves if we have enough grace to be flexible and enough humility to admit that we don't know enough to judge one another. It is a fact that Jesus also instructed us not to judge and one of His strongest teachings has to do with the necessity of forgiving one another. Without a forgiving heart, we cannot be forgiven (Matthew 18:18–35).

I have found most Christians to be far more accepting and forgiving than their legalistic leaders. I love moderate and liberal Christians because they are usually gentle in spirit. I do not enjoy mean-spirited people.

One occasion that encouraged me was the experience I shared with a fellow pastor. He was a pastor of a conservative church. He called me and told me that his wife had decided to divorce him. He did not know what would happen with the church. He was reasonably sure they would ask him to resign.

I met with the leadership of that church and talked to them about the opportunity they had to be a redemptive fellowship. It was a chance to say we really understand what it means to be forgiving. Later I met with the congregation and shared the same views with them. They later voted by an overwhelming majority to ask the pastor to stay on the job.

Less than a year later, he and his former wife were reconciled. I was privileged to perform the ceremony for their remarriage. Both the church and the pastor have more than survived. The church is stronger than ever, and the pastor stayed there with his family for several years and is still serving as a senior pastor in another state. The fact that this conservative congregation was willing to be compassionate and forgiving in this situation was a hopeful note. It is admittedly the exception, but it did happen. When grace is experienced, good things can happen.

## Women in Ministry

Yes, this is still an issue with some narrow-minded people. Some legalists will go so far as to say it is all right for women to serve in the church and church-related vocations as long as they are not ordained. I want to be benevolent, but that position seems hypocritical to me.

Should women be permitted to serve as deacons and pastors? Of course they should. Women of the Bible prophesied, preached, served, and led. Esther, Samuel's mother, Ruth, Mary, the other Mary, Phoebe, and countless others have blazed the trail alongside the men.

Mary was the first to see the resurrected Lord, the first to hear His voice after He had been raised to life again, and the first to proclaim the resurrection. Proclaiming the resurrection? That was preaching!

Ordination was not a ritualistic stamp of approval reserved for professional clergy in the early church. They ordained as an act of setting people apart for special service. The ordaining prayer was for the power of God's Spirit to rest on and in people to empower them for service. They ordained teachers, preachers, deacons, deaconesses, and missionaries. One of those designated as a female servant of the church was Phoebe (Romans 16:1). Why do we insist on straining at the gnats?

Several years ago, a woman in our congregation told me about her niece, a graduate of one of our denominational seminaries. Her niece believed that God had called her to be a minister. Her specific calling, she believed, was to be a chaplain. She could not serve as a chaplain without being ordained, but she could not find a church in the city where she obtained her seminary degree that would ordain her. Where were the expressions of grace? Legalistic grace killers were active.

Her aunt asked if we could do that. Our church was delighted to help her. We had a special ordination service for her. She then went back to her home city and became a hospital chaplain. She has continued her ministry for more than a decade. She has served in two cities as a hospital chaplain. We still get thank-you notes from her. She recently called me. In the conversation she said, "I often think of the encouragement your church gave to me. Every person I can help as a chaplain is a part of the result of your help to me." A woman in ministry! Yes, thank God!

Years ago I heard a minister explain the absence of grace in this way: "Sometimes I get the feeling that fundamentalists (legalistic Christians) are telling me that if I don't repent and believe in Christ, I am going to hell; and they seem glad that I am. A more gracious person tells me that I am going to hell if I don't repent and believe; but seems to be sorry." That is a difference between grace and legalism.

---

These are a few of the issues that could appropriately be confronted by people who are committed to accepting and sharing God's grace. Certainly, not all will agree on all the moral issues listed above. It is not agreement with one another that I am seeking. I just want us to put issues on the docket for discussion. We have the freedom to differ and still be accepted.

My personal experience has not been pleasant with legalistic church people. I do not feel the freedom to differ or even the freedom to be wrong when I am with them. I could never freely share my doubts, fears, or failures with any of the ultralegalists that I know. I can feel eyes of disapproval and hear, "Well, Bill, we will certainly pray for you." That would pretty much end the conversation unless one of them decided to help straighten me out.

I tell you, it's the absence of grace in the spirit of people that makes the major difference. There was a time when I permitted that spirit of condemnation to control me, or at least keep me from expressing my views. I do not want to live there ever again. I want to be with people who understand that we are all struggling together to understand and grow.

# GRACE, ATTITUDES, AND MINISTRY

PEOPLE WHO LIVE in the grace of God's love have an open attitude toward acceptance of others and ministry to those who are in need. Legalistic backgrounds lead to the wrong questions. When legalistic people see a blind man they might ask, "Who sinned to cause this blindness?" (John 9:1–2). Grace sees the blind man and asks, "How can we help this person?"

## Attitudes toward Poverty and Homelessness

Some people have surprised me with their beliefs that poor people and homeless people are responsible for their own conditions. They blame the victims. Legalism blames, while grace seeks to alleviate the suffering. The difference is dramatic.

I was discussing the homeless situation with a friend when he announced to me, "I am going to be honest with you. I don't believe anyone has any excuse to be homeless. If they really want to, those people can find work and a place to live."

My response was, "Are you suggesting that people want to be homeless?"

He said, "I can't think of any other explanation. Why do you think they are in the mess they are in?"

I said, "I believe that it started a long time before the present generation. If you are born into a poor family, you probably won't get an education. You simply can't afford it. You have not learned any other way. I have talked to people who are caught in that trap, and I know that they sincerely want to get out." We never came to any agreement on the issue, but I thought of our discussion when I read an article in a local newspaper on homelessness. The article noted that the principle cause of homelessness is poverty and a lack of affordable housing.

It also noted that children under twelve years of age make up the largest segment of the homeless population in this country.

I remembered the comment about blaming the homeless for their condition when I read of a woman and her two children who were staying in a homeless shelter. This woman said, "This shelter is not a home. I'm out there looking for a job, and I'll find one." She added, "I'm smart. I graduated high school. I have experience. I just need a chance. The shelter has been a real lifesaver, but my children need a home." She is homeless, but it would be more than insensitive to blame her for that condition.

While some politicians want to cut aid to such people, many innocent children continue to suffer. I only wish we could do more.

The fact is that poor people, with little education and training, are stuck in menial and minimum-wage jobs. No one is going to climb out of poverty on minimum wages. Most of those minimum-wage jobs have zero benefits. All it takes is one serious illness, and the family is so far under that they will never get out without help.

It is sad but true, as author George Lakoff points out the upper- and middle-class people need people on that lower level of employment so we can have house cleaners, quick meals at a drive-through, and inexpensive child care. Unconsciously, a society that needs people in those jobs continues to contribute to the problem. That is an immoral situation or so it seems to those who would extend grace to the poor.

A few years ago a young woman came to our church. She was seventeen years old and already had four children. When I asked her about her pregnancies, she told me that family members had repeatedly raped her. She had three children by an uncle and two older cousins. The fourth was a result of a male friend of her uncle's who came into her bedroom late one night and forced her into a sexual encounter.

She was literally begging for help. She wanted to be a practical nurse, but how was she to get training? How could she care for her children and get the necessary training to get out of that sick family situation?

We were able to provide childcare for her while she received training through a government program. The happy ending to that story is that she became a practical nurse and was able to support her children. Last I heard she was living a productive life and raising her children away from the horrid environment where she had grown up.

Not everyone is as fortunate as she was. We saw homeless people regularly at our church. We fed hundreds each year, but that is just a drop in the bucket of needs. My experience has been that people who know they have received grace from God are more likely to be compassionate and far less likely to blame the victim for the circumstance. That woman was the recipient of God's outrageous and wonderful grace because there were people who believed in that grace who were willing to help her.

## The Major Difference in the Two Moralities

This is another overly generalized statement, but I believe that the basic difference between the morality of compassion and morality of legalism is the difference between law and grace. It is the difference between legalism and compassion. One way to understand that difference is that *legalism* says, "Obey these laws and you shall live." *Grace* says, "When you have the life of Christ in you, there will never be any condemnation for you. You are at liberty to help and accept others as you have been accepted."

## The Tale of Two Churches

There were two churches in the city. One of them was easily identified as an extremely legalistic congregation. The other was a gracious group that was called liberal by the first congregation. The two pastors knew each other and were cordial but not close friends by any means.

The pastor of the first church was known as a strong fundamentalist preacher. He was what many refer to as a fire-and-brimstone preacher. He was clearly legalistic in his interpretation of the Scriptures. His church flourished and was held in high esteem by denominational leaders in the area.

The pastor of the second church was known as a theological moderate. He included in his messages issues like racial relations, the homeless, as well as strong focus on the other teachings of Jesus in the New Testament. His church struggled.

The first church had strong Sunday school attendance and two revivals every year. They were a strong evangelistic congregation; at least, the pastor was evangelistic in his focus.

The second church had an average attendance in their services. They were strong in ministries. They regularly provided space for homeless people, food for poverty-stricken people, and reached out to international students.

The first church had compassion for lost souls. There is nothing wrong with that at all.

The second church had compassion. Christian compassion must go beyond concern for saving souls. It must also be concerned about saving lives.

In the passing of time both pastors experienced divorce. Neither instigated divorce, but privately both admitted that the failure in their marriages was a shared responsibility between them and their spouses.

There was no discussion about the decision concerning retention of the pastor in the first church. His ministry was over. He vacated his office the week after the announcement that a divorce was coming. He is now a shoe salesman.

In the second church, the minister announced to the congregation that his wife was divorcing him. He said that in order to spare the church embarrassment, he would resign. When that announcement was made, a man stood in the back of the congregation. He said, "Wait a minute. I am divorced, and I am here because you told me that divorce did not disqualify me from serving in this church. Why would the same not be true for you?" Another stood and repeated essentially the same message. After a moment of silence, a deacon stood and said, "Let's have a special meeting of the deacons and discuss this situation with our pastor." That meeting was held the following Saturday morning.

The deacons met first and then invited the pastor in. He was not asked to speak. The chairman simply reported to him the decision of the group. He said, "We have decided to ask you to take a couple of months off to recover. During that time you are to pray about what you believe you should do. If you decide that you honestly believe that God wants you to leave this church, we will accept that. Just know this: we will not accept your resignation on the basis of your divorce. You have taught here that God's grace permits people to serve even after a divorce."

That pastor left for a two-month sabbatical and returned on Easter Sunday morning. He drove onto the church parking lot where trees were decorated with yellow ribbons. There was a yellow ribbon on his office door. There was a yellow ribbon on the door to the sanctuary.

He could not restrain the tears when he returned to the pulpit and said he would stay. He remained as pastor of that congregation until he retired.

There is a difference in spirit between those two churches. If you visit the first, you find an atmosphere of dissention. In the second, you find a warm acceptance. That is the difference between compassionate and grace-filled morality and legalistic morality.

Both are Christian churches, but they come to the expression of their faith from different perspectives. Legalism can be devastating if you are the recipient of its ironclad judgment. I do not like legalistic religion whether it is Christian, Jewish, or Moslem. I like moderate, kind-hearted people, and I like religion of grace, like that of Jesus.

## The Real Demon Is the Idea and the Attitudes Produced by the Idea

I indicated earlier in this discussion that ideology is the real culprit. Before you embrace an ideology, take a look at what it leads to. Never get on a plane if you don't know where it is going. I have persisted in demonstrating the destination of ultraconservative and legalistic ideology. If strongly adhered to, it becomes legalistic, harsh, judgmental, and mean-spirited. I don't want to go there! Legalists seem to be driven by the desire for authority that will give them a sense of security. Ultimately that search is shipwrecked on the shores of reality. There is no security outside our faith and personal relationship to a God of grace and love.

Long ago I heard a comment that is worth repeating: "We are not to be judges but there is nothing wrong with being fruit inspectors." Jesus said, "By their fruit you will know them" (know them, not judge them). If the fruit is bad, the tree is bad. The fruit of legalistic religion (grounded in law and rules) looks bad to me.

A problem in discussing morality is that the concept of morals changes, at least the legalistic morality does. One of the interracial couples in our church recently reminded me that less than two decades ago, their relationship was not only considered immoral but also illegal in some places. If violating laws is immoral, we have to take a long look at our legal system. Some of it is outdated and unfair.

The banner of grace needs to be lifted high above our heads and the truth of grace ground into our hearts. This can lead to compassionate attitudes and acceptance of struggling people into the fold of God's outrageous grace.

# RUSTY PIPES AND LIVING WATER

WHO OF US is worthy of delivering the message of the gospel? None of us is worthy. We say these words but often still believe that maybe we are at least qualified as much as anyone else could be. As long as I sinned in things like a little greed, a few or several lustful thoughts, stretching the truth a little bit, or even making judgments on people with whom I disagree and as long as more serious sins were private, I did not really recognize my unworthiness.

The truth is that when I first began my preaching ministry I had trouble not believing that I was another Bill Graham, or at least a Norman Vincent Peale. I became focused more on the messenger than on the message. I read in John 7:35 that Jesus said, "Whoever believes in me, as the Scripture has said, streams of living water will flow from within him." I pictured myself as a conduit for the living water and felt pretty good about that role.

A few years ago after some failures from twenty-five to thirty or so years ago were made public, I felt unworthy. In my prayer one night, I said, "God, I know that I am no longer worthy to continue in your service." It was almost as if an audible voice was ringing in my head, "You arrogant jerk, who told you that you were ever worthy?" I don't think God really called me a jerk, but it sounded like it might have been his call. I could not disagree and then realized how much I had always been dependent on His grace.

At my best, I am still sinful. My motives are even tainted. I want to do something good for others, but it is almost impossible for me not to hope my good deeds will be noticed and credited to me by the people around me if not by God.

I am a sinner and certainly have not earned any rights to serve God and deliver his message, but He has graciously permitted me to do that anyway. Remembering the passage from John's Gospel, I told friends that I deliver living water (the gospel) through rusty pipes. Still, the water is good. Paul said it this way: "We have this treasure [the gospel] in earthen vessels." I keep on trying to get the rust out but some remains. Only by the grace of God can I continue to deliver the living water.

We are wise to see that we live in an imperfect world and that we are all imperfect. If we could just trot one perfect person out of the masses, grace would be dead, but that is not going to happen. We are utterly dependent on God's grace.

The concept is not new. Drunks help drunks (read of AA). Sinners help sinners. That is our only hope. Still, all the help we get is ultimately from our God.

My grandmother used to tell me a story of a poor woman who really wanted a turkey for Christmas. She could not possibly afford one, so she started praying every night for God to send her a turkey. Two rowdy boys were walking by her window and heard her prayer. They decided it would be fun to get a turkey and drop it down her chimney. They did. The woman found the turkey and began thanking God for the gift of a Christmas turkey. The boys again heard her praying and stuck their heads in the window. They said, "God didn't send that turkey. We brought it and dropped it down your chimney." She responded, saying, "God sent it even if he used the devil to deliver it."

God sends His gifts and messages through rusty pipes and earthen vessels.

Remember that it is the message and not the messenger that is vital. The apostle Paul was confronted with people who he said preached the gospel out of envy and at times got him into trouble or as he said that they caused him distress. The passage in Philippians 1:12–20 makes it clear that Paul believed the important thing was that the gospel message be preached. The motives of the messenger were not important as long as Gospel is still being preached.

We who preach sometimes overestimate our own importance in the process of delivering the gospel to our congregations. We are earthen vessels holding a valuable treasure. We are not the treasure; the message of good news about God's grace is the treasure. The conduit may be rusty, but it is the living water that is important.

The preacher's life may be far from exemplary, his or her motives impure or mixed, but the message can still be powerful and life changing for hearers.

Does that mean that we should not be concerned about our lives and motives? Certainly not! We should strive to be the best vessels possible and the cleanest pipes or conduits for the living water as possible. The point is that the outrageous grace of God can make use of our lives and messages regardless of our imperfections.

A person dying of thirst would drink water from a dirty cup. A person dying of hunger would eat bread delivered by unclean hands. Hungry and needy souls can be redeemed and fed by imperfect people.

My view of myself as another Billy Graham or Norman Vincent Peale has been altered. I now see myself as a man who has been given God's grace and enabled to deliver the most important message in the world. I am blessed and honored but not deserving of this opportunity.

I do not know that I will ever have a chance to preach the gospel again, but if I do, I will gladly do it. If God's grace gives me the gift of that opportunity, I will make the most of it that I can, but if I do not have that opportunity, I will accept the fact that God's grace is sufficient for either eventuality (2 Corinthians 12:9).

To any others who feel like they would like to deliver a message of grace but they simply are not worthy to do so, I say this: of course, you are not worthy. None of us are. But the important thing is not your or my worthiness but our faithfulness in delivering the message that is so desperately needed.

The people to whom we deliver the message are unworthy too, but God loves them and wants to lift them up. Out of our unworthiness to their unworthiness we say, "There is hope for us all." I like the definition of preaching the gospel as one hungry person bringing food to other hungry people.

Recognizing our own imperfections and realizing that we are recipients of God's outrageous grace gives us a chance to share hope to depressed and discouraged people. God loves us all and is willing to extend his grace to anyone who is willing to receive it or as Manning has said, "None of us have fallen so far that God cannot use us in his service."

We will never reach perfection in this world. We need grace.

# FREE BUT NOT FORCED

GRACE IS FREE, but it is not forced on anyone. We can have it if we believe in it and are willing to receive it, but it is not forced on those who do not want it or even believe in it.

There were two thieves who died on crosses next to the crucified Jesus. One of them asked for grace with a simple request, "Lord, remember me when you come into your kingdom." Jesus extended grace to him, saying, "Today you will be with me in paradise." No such gift was extended to the other man dying that day. The same grace was available to both men, but only one asked and was willing to receive it.

Not only is it not forced on us, we are not to presume on that grace. When I was in seminary I remember hearing one preacher say, "Some people act like they have God nailed to a cross, and they can, therefore, do anything they want." Those who believe that are simply making a terrible misrepresentation of the truth. Such a statement ignores the fact that because of the death of Jesus, grace is available to all of us, but it is not automatic. While we cannot work our way into God's forgiving love, we can, by faith, accept it.

Few of the Pharisees received God's grace. They arrogantly thought that they didn't need it. They assumed that they had the right pedigree and the right doctrine. It is not the right pedigree, denomination, doctrinal creeds, or even good works that bring us into a right relationship with God. It is our willingness to accept the outrageous grace of God by faith.

I said *few* concerning the Pharisees. There were exceptions among the religious leaders of the Jews, but they were the exceptions. Anyone could have received God's grace, but many did not. God does not force himself on His children. He responds to our requests to Him, but He doesn't read our mail without invitation.

One of the most dramatic pictures of Jesus comes from Revelation 3:20. Here, Jesus is seen standing at the door, knocking and saying that if anyone will open the door and invite him in, He will enter. He will knock at the door but only comes in if we open the door.

One of my friends told me that legalistic people try to take the kingdom of God by force. They are going to work hard enough and do enough good deeds or give enough money to be accepted into the kingdom of God. They wrestle with God in prayer but miss the point that Jesus came to offer a light yoke and an easy way. He was gentle in His invitations to those who were in greatest need, but He never was heavy-handed in presenting grace.

What I am saying is that your marriage to God is not going to be a shotgun marriage. You are invited but not forced. Receiving grace for living your life for God is the greatest opportunity in the world, why would anyone not willingly accept it?

Starving people can sit at a table loaded with food and still starve unless they are willing to eat. You will not be forced to eat, but it is available. Eating is a choice and so is starving when food is available. Eat and share the food with other hungry people.

I was in college and played basketball with a jovial fellow who would invite teammates to come to his house and enjoy a visit anytime they wanted. He invited us with the statement, "Come on down to my house. The door is unlocked and Kool-Aid and cookies are sitting on the table." It was an open invitation, but no one was forced to go. I never went and often have wondered if there really was Kool-Aid and cookies on his table. I'll never know because I didn't accept the invitation. Don't make that mistake about the grace of God. It is available to you. God's door is open to you, and food is on the table. Come on in.

# FRUSTRATION AND PERFECTION

FRUSTRATION. STARTING TO do something that is good and getting sidetracked doing something that is bad, that is a common frustration of people who have decided to live the Christian life. Probably the most familiar example of this frustration is found in the Romans 7 and referred to earlier in this manuscript. Here, the apostle Paul says that he intends to do good things but then does the things that he had not intended. He means well, he says, but winds up doing wrong.

What is the problem? Paul and all of us are victims of imperfection. We are all imperfect. It does not come as a surprise to us when after a mistake, someone says, "Well, I am not perfect." No kidding! Perfection is an illusion in this world. This is an imperfect world occupied by imperfect people. We keep looking but do not find those perfect things.

Jerry Coleman, who was a baseball announcer for the San Diego Padres, is credited with saying, "We have a perfect day here at Sun City Stadium and we are expecting an even more perfect day tomorrow." Though we know that perfect is not possible, we continue to dream of it.

We look for utopia. Even the word should stop us. It literally means no place. We get the word from a book by Sir Thomas Moore by that title written in 1516. It was a book about a perfect place. The Greek *ou* means "no." *Topos* means "place." It is an imaginary island representing the perfect society. It simply does not exist. When we look for utopia, we are looking for no place.

Shangri-la is another fictional place in the book *Lost Horizons* by James Hilton and described as a mystical harmonious valley, gently guided from a lamasery enclosed in the western end of the Kunhun Mountains. It has become synonymous with any earthly paradise. It is the vision of a place where people live free from imperfections and secure from the outside world. The problem is that it does not exist.

People who know these are fiction still have their own ideas of an idyllic kingdom of heaven where perfection exists. Again, the fact is that even when such a state exists, it only exists in a spiritual way and never as a part of this material world. We simply are not going to find perfection in this life.

Reality is that we imperfect people will continue to live imperfect lives for as long as this world exists. This includes *all* of us.

This is not meant to become an excuse for failures in our lives. We are responsible for being the best people and we cannot beg off because of our imperfections. Living in an imperfect world does not remove our responsibility. We are plagued with the sickness of "I can't help it." One of the first lessons we learn is that when we do something wrong, it is someone else's fault. That is not the point of facing the reality of imperfection. We are responsible, and we need grace.

Some object that Jesus told us to be perfect. Yes, He did say that, but when He said it, He did not use a word that meant moral perfection. He used a word that meant being what we are intended to be.

Barclay points out that the Greek word translated "perfect" is the word *teleios*. It is a word that has nothing to do with abstract, philosophical, metaphysical, or moral perfection.

In the sense of the word Jesus used, a man is perfect (telios) when he is full-grown in contradistinction to a half-grown boy. A student who has reached a mature knowledge of his study is telios as compared to a student who is beginning to study.

This concept of perfection is best seen as becoming what we are intended to be. In that sense, we are being perfect when we are doing the things that we are meant to do. If someone is meant to be a singer, that person is being perfect when he/she is singing. A bird is perfect in this sense just because it is being a bird. It is not, however, being a perfect bird! We must live with it! We are not going to find perfection in this world.

The pursuit of perfection can be a healthy drive leading to improvement. We can live better though imperfect lives. If aiming at perfection leads to self-improvement, it can be an asset. On the other hand, it is possible to become so obsessed with perfection that what could have been a stepping stone becomes a stumbling block that leads to destruction.

I heard recently of a golfer who became so obsessed with hitting perfect golf shots that he began to spend an inordinate amount of time playing and practicing golf. He lost his job, and his wife and family left him.

When he was interviewed about the situation, he said that when he hit even one near-perfect golf shot, the feeling was so good that he wanted to experience it again and again. He compared it to a high that leads drug addicts to go back again and again to drugs to seek that feeling.

I have known of Christian people who became so obsessed with the pursuit of perfection that they completely lost touch with reality. They practically became hermits, withdrawing from normal contact with life. One such person was a minister who wanted not only to become the perfect person but wanted his children to be perfect. He saw attending movies as an imperfection and, on at least one occasion, literally tied one of his children to a chair to keep him from attending a movie.

Years later after his son grew up with serious behavioral problems, the minister said that if he had known then what he had now learned, he would have gone to the movie with his son. They could have talked about it later.

Whether the desire for perfection is a healthy motivation to do better or an addiction that leads to a destructive lifestyle, it is still not going to be achieved. We are imperfect, and this is an imperfect world. As much as I may want to live a totally consistent life for God, I cannot.

I can do better, but I have stumbled in and out of the Christian standards for life so many times that my "repenter" is almost worn out. Still, I need repentance every day of my imperfect life.

One of my spiritual mentors, Rolland Brown, told me that all of us may live in the kingdom of God, but we will move in and out of that kingdom often. He said that the goal is to continue coming back to that relationship every time we fail or fall. He told me that there were times he would get up in the morning in the kingdom of God, thanking Him with every step he took until he got to the breakfast table and found that the toast had been burned. His only hope and ours is grace.

Simon Peter proclaimed that Jesus was the Son of God. Jesus told him that he had spoken a revelation from God. In that moment, Peter was surely *in* the kingdom of God. A short time later, after Jesus told his disciples that, he would have to go to Jerusalem and suffer at the hands of men, Peter said that was not going to happen. Jesus told Peter that he was speaking thoughts from evil and not from God. Obviously, Peter was now not in but *out* of the kingdom of God. Peter then clearly stood in the need of grace (Matthew 16).

This in-and-out life led me to pursue a more consistent life. I began a search for such a life more than fifty years ago. I will describe some of that search in the next chapter, but I will tell you now that after a half a century of searching, I came to the conclusion that it is all about grace. I am so imperfect that I will always need the grace of God in my life.

Grace is the unmerited favor we receive from God. It is what bridges the gap between what we are and what we could be if we did everything right. It is the only hope for eternal life and for strength to persevere through the tough times. The good news is that it is available to us. I need that grace every day, and I thank God for it.

This is important because it may be a common desire to somehow reach the ideal life, the ideal state of existence. Even when we acknowledge that it is an impossible dream for this world, we hold on to the desire with hope that it will be achieved in a future life in eternity.

Many look for a perfect church. Have you ever wondered what a perfect church might be like? I have. I wondered until I started thinking about who the members would be. Imagine composing a church of the great leaders listed in the Bible. No disrespect is intended in the following notations, just thinking about the fact that not even leaders from the Bible could form a perfect church.

We could start with Abraham. He is the father of our faith (Hebrews). He could be a foundation stone in the perfect church. The only problem is that despite of his great faith, he lied about Sarah being his wife in order to protect himself. He struggled with human sacrifice. He was no doubt a good—even great—man, but he was not perfect.

King David would make a good worship leader and could write and lead us in devotional thoughts. Look at the Psalms. Still, he was far from perfection. As noted in chapter 1, he, after being selected as king of Israel and being anointed as God's chosen one, committed adultery and murder among other things. He was a good and great man, but he was certainly not perfect.

Jacob could be a business administrator and chair the ethics committee. He was a deceiver and tricked his brother out of his birthright, but he is one of the heroes of faith. He is just imperfect like the rest of us.

Simon Peter could be pastor of such a church, but as indicated above, he was in and out of harmony with Jesus. He even vowed never to desert Jesus no matter what happened, but he denied Jesus three times after that. He was a good and great man, but he was not perfect.

Rahab could be a leader of women's organizations because she was selected to help Israel win a city and to be in the lineage of Jesus, but she was a prostitute. She was a good woman and accepted as an ancestor of Jesus, but she was not perfect.

The list could go on. While none of these people are anymore perfect than we are, they should all be accepted by us as fellow pilgrims. We are all prodigals and need to create an atmosphere of honesty and grace so we can get on with the job of serving God to the best of our ability. We cannot find perfect people to lean on even from the Bible, so why don't we just accept the fact that we are all imperfect and start just being more realistic about our lives and needs?

We are all inconsistent. We are inconsistent even when we mean well. When I say that we are all inconsistent, I mean that we are all in and out of the kingdom of God. For me, the kingdom of God is a state of love and peace. It is achieved when we live in the Spirit of God or when we live with a heart of peace.

My dream is to live life in the kingdom of God. I know that the possibility for that life must be real, but I have not even experienced it consistently. The fact is that I am up and down, in and out, back and forth, and just about every other contradiction that you can name. I suspect that is the experience of others who are seeking greater spiritual depth. That includes a myriad of people.

It is probably the experience of Hindus and Buddhists who seek to achieve nirvana, a state of bliss or peace and a state that can be experienced in life or may be entered into in death. It is every person's Shangri-La or utopia. It is the hope of many that such a place or state is attainable on this earth and that Shangri-La and utopia are just as real as they hope the kingdom of God can be real on this earth. There we can find happiness, fulfillment, joy, and peace forever, but we hedge our bets by noting that if we do not find these in this world, perhaps we can live in such a way or believe in such a way that we will find them forever in the afterlife. It is the ultimate kingdom of God sought by Christians. Jesus even taught his followers to "seek first the Kingdom of God and his righteousness and all the other things needed would be given to them" (Matthew 6:33). Sought, but not achieved.

It is possibly this same desire for happiness and peace that sometimes drives addicts to come back again and again to the high they experience when on drugs. It is not the desire that is the problem. It is the methods used to seek to satisfy the desire that becomes problematic. Perhaps the failure to achieve high levels of security, happiness, and peace is the reason for so much frustration in our lives.

There is a tremendous gap between our realizations and our dreams. We think that we can find a way to fulfill those dreams and be inwardly happy and at peace in our homes, jobs, and lives. Note that I said *inwardly*. I do not believe that what we seek can be found as a literal place in this world but must be found—if it is to be found at all—inside of us, in our own hearts and minds. Jesus taught, "The Kingdom of God is in your midst" (Luke 17:21).

We fail to find this to be our permanent experience, but we keep on seeking. At least, that is what I have done in my life. If such a state exists, I want to find it. I read the books that make the promises, and I keep on seeking, believing, that if I seek, I shall find. All I have found are hints and small approximations of the dream. Maybe that is all I will ever find.

At my very best, I find myself in and out of the ideal existence over and over again. That is the theme of what I am writing in this book. It is about the pursuit, the failures, the frustrations, and the continuing hope to live more consistently in harmony with the best urges of my heart.

I keep hoping for the experience of living a life in the spirit as described in Galatians 5. I keep hoping for the experience of living in the kingdom of God and living life that is totally like the life of Christ. I still have not found it as a permanent or consistent thing in my life. I believe that is a common frustration of fellow seekers. I write this material for all of us who have sought but not found our utopia.

While I cannot promise that you can live a perfect life in the kingdom of God consistently, I can promise you that you never need to fall outside the circle of God's outrageous grace and love.

Many of us desire to live a life that expresses mercy, love, forgiveness, grace, kindness, and unselfishness. It means turning the other cheek (not seeking revenge when offended) and going the extra mile (doing more than is expected of us). It especially means seeking to help others alleviate their suffering and pain (seeking justice and peace). It is doing unto others what you would have them do unto you, loving others as you love yourself, and loving God with all your heart and mind and soul. It is focusing on pure thoughts and positive thoughts, accepting others where they are, and trying to help them get to where they need to go. In general, it would be living a life of respect, reverence, and love toward God and others. When you live like this, you will be living in God's grace and love.

Living in the heart of peace is defined by the authors of *The Anatomy of Peace* as living from a heart that views others as people, people who have the same hopes, fears, and needs that become as real to me as my own. The heart of war they say is to view others as objects, obstacles, vehicles, and irrelevancies. In the words of Stephen Covey, author of *The 7 Habits of Highly Effective People*, the heart of peace is the heart that seeks first to understand and then to be understood.

Are we trusting in the grace of God daily? That is the question we all have to answer for ourselves. It is a question that is becoming vital in my own life. Thank God for His wonderful grace.

# I HAVE RECEIVED
# OUTRAGEOUS GRACE

After reading Paul's experience when he was writing the book of Romans and struggling with his own sinful nature, I wondered if this was his confession or his testimony. Confessions are admissions of our sins and accepting responsibility for them. Testimony is sharing victorious experience from our lives of faith. What I am sharing now is both confession and testimony.

Paul's experience found in Romans 7 is both. It is confession of sin and a statement of victory in his faith that God could deliver him from his sinful behavior.

I decided after reflecting on Paul's writing that I would share some of my confessions and then end the sharing with a testimony of victory in the Grace of God. I was also motivated to share when I read the following statement from Fil Anderson's book *Breaking the Rules*. He said, "My highest hope is for all of us to stop trying to fool others by appearing to have our act together. As people living in intimate union with God we need to become better known for what and who we really are."

Anderson adds a sobering statement: "Perhaps a good place to begin would be telling the world—before the world does its own investigation—that we are not as bad as they think. We are worse. At least I know that I'm worse.... Let's get real." Now, I want to get real.

For fifty-one years I served as senior pastor of a wonderful congregation at Christ Memorial Baptist Church. We were all recipients of God's grace. We were a congregation of sinners saved by God's grace (Ephesians 2:8–9). Together we accomplished some wonderful things. Mind you, we accomplished them by the grace of God.

I preached and led the church for that entire fifty-one years even though on many days the good and the evil thoughts were lying down together in my mind. I truly related to Paul's struggle described in Romans 7.

For example, I served as senior pastor of a church for fifty-one years. During that time I struggled with several problems, the most dramatic of which was sensual and inappropriate sexual behaviors. That was going on while I was really trying to reach a deeper level of commitment to God. I was a recipient of the outrageous grace of God. To some degree, that is true of every one of us, but I can only share from my own experience. Still, I know it is not unique. Below is an example from one of my journals in 1963.

July 17, 1963

Last night something happened to me. I was sleeping in a room by myself. I was awakened by a feeling that is hard to describe. There were waves of heat that flowed through my whole body. I wish I had been fully awake when it began because no one could believe that I partially dreamed this, for I have read of such things happening to others. My whole body was tingling, and I know I was awake. I felt to see if anyone else was in the bed with me.

Then I realized that God was doing that to me. I said, "Please don't stop." As the sensation grew stronger I wanted to shout, "Hallelujah," and I did, but though I gave as much volume as I could to it, it stayed in my throat. I wanted to speak but couldn't. Then I heard something. I thought the phone rang. Someone was in the room with me. I assumed it was my wife standing by the dresser. I said, "Did I wake you?"

The sensations stopped, and I looked up but no one was there. I felt the bed again, and sure enough I was alone. I know I was on the verge of a deeper experience with the spirit of God.

I must say I'm somewhat confused. I am not worthy of God's blessings though I want them very much. I am a very weak person, and sex has always been a tremendous temptation to me. It still is today. I want to have Jesus fill my heart, but I know this lust must go. I've prayed much about it but have too often fed it with thoughts and yielding. I wonder what I'd do if real opportunity came. Yet I don't want this feeling in me. I confess it, and I know God forgives me. I am just waiting to see what else happens.

Now, I am going to begin a stricter discipline of myself and my time and try to do at least four things: (1) set aside time for Bible study, prayer, and meditation; (2) witness to lost people at least one afternoon a week and more if the Spirit leads me; (3) cultivate people who want the same experience such as Rondal Fisher, Paul Smith, and Roger Barnard; (4) spend devotional time with my family.

I know this doesn't sound like much, but when I add church administration, committees, etc., sick people to visit, general pastoral duties like weddings and the like, and recreation, it will require strict discipline. Of course, there must be time for sermon preparation.

I'll keep a close record of my progress.

For almost twenty years from that night, I kept journals by writing a prayer every day. I included two scripture passages and thoughts on them then added specific prayers each day. I almost always added a poem at the end of the day's thoughts. I still have many of the journals and most of the poetry.

My life was moving quickly, and unbelievable things were happening. I will list only a few of them. I finished my seminary education the next year. I then completed a master's degree in counseling at Southern Illinois University in Edwardsville, Illinois. I completed a PhD in counseling at Washington University in St. Louis and did a research study on the effect of several counseling interventions on cancer patients in treatment at Barnes Hospital in St. Louis.

I taught a class in marriage and family therapy at Washington University's school of social work. I did a regular on air counseling program at KMOX Radio in St. Louis and published my first book, *This Will Drive You Sane*.

During that time, I began speaking at various companies and organizations all over the United States and began working with the Cardinals baseball team. My counseling load was growing out of control, and I was still serving as the senior pastor of Christ Memorial Baptist Church.

The church I served was made up of a wonderful group of people who were unusually flexible and accepting. We were an unusual Baptist church where women were accepted in ministry and ordained, we joined an African American convention to make a statement on race relations and remained active in that area. We accepted divorced people to serve in any position available in the church. We formally accepted the disease concept of alcoholism and started support groups. We established benevolent ministries to the hungry. We were one of the first three churches in Missouri to join the newly formed Cooperative Baptist Fellowship. We supported a myriad of ministries and had a great family relationship within the church.

In addition to the other activities in my life, my wife Teresa Gay and I founded and operated the Cancer Support Center of St. Louis during these years and over a ten-year period saw and helped more than 1,500 cancer patients and their families.

With all this going on, one would think that my spiritual life was strong and in many respects it was, but it was also inconsistent. While I was devoting myself to prayer and attempting to follow God in my life, I was also at times involved in inappropriate relationships. Sex was not the only problem but a major problem. Facing that issue was a constant struggle for me. I can thank God that after a year in therapy and continuing support therapy, that problem has not been a part of my life for more than a quarter of a century. In the terms of Alcoholics Anonymous, "I have not fallen off the wagon for twenty-four years." There are certainly plenty of other inconsistencies in my life, but that one has been gone for a long time.

One of my deepest regrets during the earlier period of my life was the disintegration of my family life. I spent far too little time with my children. I love them with my whole heart, but I failed them miserably by being absent. My marriage also failed. My first wife and I were divorced in 1992.

One of the other inconsistencies in my life was a gradual addiction to gambling. Having overcome one problem, I developed another one. I lost considerable amounts of money before my wife, Teresa, convinced me that I was addicted. I stopped that addiction by the grace of God. I am being as honest as I can about my life because through it all, I have walked in the circle of God's grace and love.

I am sure that I am not alone in my struggles, and I hope my confessions and testimony to the broad, based love and grace of God can be an encouragement to others. To aid in that attempt, I have written several books, all but two were written after my therapies were started. Among them is a book titled *The First Stone*. It further chronicles my own struggles and offers hope to others who are facing similar issues.

Since we all completely need the grace of God every day, it should come as no surprise to us when we recognize inconsistencies in the lives of others. The apostle Paul is clearly one who struggled with this same issue. Read

Romans 7. Paul here shares that he fought with the reality that he did things he knew were wrong and failed to do things he knew were right. He was speaking in the present tense. He was a Christian, but he still fought with inconsistency. Don't we all? Again, please put emphasis on *all*. Don't miss the universality of this truth and need.

I have regurgitated a whole pile of paradoxes and inconsistencies that I have experienced, and I am still afraid that some people will read the beginning of the story and stop without finishing it. Part of me fears to risk that, but a lot of me really believes it is vital—not only to me but to others—to run the risk and at least begin. Hiding our flaws from one another is a destructive habit and needs to be challenged.

I don't ever want to hide my faith either. I am free to admit that I believe in God's love and grace, but in order for that to be real, I don't want to hide my flaws either.

This desire to share was rekindled recently when I reread Brennen Manning's book *It Is All Grace* and when I reread some of my journaling from some fifty-two years ago.

Manning pictures for us a scene from the Old Testament in which Samson is blinded and his captors have chained him to two pillars that hold up the building they are in. Samson's strength had returned and he pulled the pillars down and destroyed the building and all who were in it. I really identify with what he says next, "With whatever strength I have left I would like to grab the chains and pull one last time. I have no delusions about heroically bringing down the house of fear that imprisons so many. My desire is to witness, nothing else."

His witness is to a message that he has preached for more than fifty years. That message is that God loves unconditionally as we are and not as we should be because none of us are as we should be. This is the message of real grace, and it is granted through Jesus Christ. I doubt that I or anyone of us really comprehends the depth and reach of this grace though we live in and by it every day and are eternally saved by it.

In order to understand that grace, we have to understand the truth about ourselves and all people around us. We have to stand before the truth, stripped of all cover and pretense. We have to confess our imperfections and share our insights when possible. All must be done without hypocrisy. That is a tall order, but it is essential to understanding the grace of God.

Manning said that he was a notorious sinner still he blessed the lives of thousands. His is an incredible story of the redemptive power of God's grace. His story is my story as well, and probably, if you are willing, you can relate.

We live with a delusion that spiritual leaders cannot be inconsistent in their lives. That is clearly a delusion. We can all easily get caught up in it. When that happens, we lose our grip on reality and become unreal in our expectations

Bill Little

of ourselves and others. It is a delusion because there are no perfect people or as the apostle Paul wrote, "All have sinned and come short of God's Glory." We can correctly add "have sinned" and "continue to sin." None of us live totally consistent lives.

I knew a minister who was renowned for telling tall tales and claiming that they were true. Bluntly, he was a liar. Still, he was accepted in churches and served as a pastor in spite of his considerable and known sins. Another minister with far less inconsistency but who was guilty of involvement in an affair was completely rejected by churches even after confession and repentance. I guess his sin was not as forgivable as lying. We certainly have invented a hierarchy of sins.

I was in a meeting of local ministers several years ago. It was announced in that meeting that a pastor in a neighboring state had stolen funds donated for a children's home. He took the money and left the country. After a few minutes of sharing thoughts about how terrible that was, one man said, "Well, at least he was not guilty of immorality." Not guilty of immorality? Does that mean that he had not committed a sexual sin and that the man separates sin into *awful*, *bad*, and *not so bad*? It seems to me that stealing money that was intended to help homeless children is a fairly *bad* sin and certainly borders on *awful*. It seems to fall under the designation *immoral*.

122

Most of us hesitate to tell the truth about our lives because we think we are so different from others. I have come to believe that we are all in this mess together. There is so much good in the worst of us and so much bad in the best of us that it hardly behooves any of us to talk about the rest of us.

No one has fallen beyond the grace of God. In Manning's words, "Grace is sufficient even though we huff and puff with all our might to try to find something or someone it cannot cover. Grace is enough. He is enough. Jesus is enough." I thank God!

Grace has allowed me to continue my service to God. Every time I have failed and been blocked from serving God, another door has opened and service continues. I wonder why he continues to use me in his service then I remember that Paul noted that we have this message in earthen vessels or as I said earlier, "The living water flows through rusty pipes."

Some of my flaws have been publicized. Newspaper stories have been written about some of my failures. Though they contained some misinformation and exaggeration, they were true enough to reveal real problems in my life. I don't know if I would have ever been open about some of these things as I was forced to be, but I can see that it was a good thing for me and can be used as good for others.

Repeated redemption of God is experience by all of us. As I said above, every time one door is closed another opens. God's grace is always sufficient, and there is no limit to His grace and forgiveness.

Grace is characterized by the extreme love of God and by forgiveness. Jesus told his disciples that they were to forgive not seven times but seventy times. Trust in God and a life of loving God, self, and others demands regular forgiveness to others and to ourselves.

Lawsuits filed against me were for what I did twenty-five and thirty years ago, not what I am doing at the present. What I did was wrong, and I cannot excuse any of that, but I did try to overcome it and went through a thorough process to deal with it more than twenty years ago.

I still believe in the redemptive power and grace of God. I know that God is willing to use me in his service, and that may happen but not without resistance. I understand the resistance but do not agree with it. We need to be more gracious with people who have fallen. After all, but for the grace of God, any of us can fall.

Are you filled with grace? Would you be willing for me to come and speak in your church fellowship? Few would. I know that is true and understand part of that but still pray that I may find grace among some of my Christian friends and fellow prodigals.

This is not a call for baring all souls.

I may have shared too much of my life but not all of it. I am not suggesting that we all need to tell others about all our imperfections. My hope is for more integrity in all our lives. It would do little, if any good, for everyone to bare their lives to the public. What we can do is acknowledge that we are all in this life together and we can stop harshly judging one another.

At the same time, I know that there are multitudes of people who have a lot that they could confess. Just be aware of that and don't come down too hard on those who have confessed or are known to have serious imperfections (maybe there is no other kind).

I heard of a woman who divorced her husband, had an abortion, moved in with a young man, broke up with him, moved in with another man, and they later married. One more abortion and then they went back into an active relationship with a church. They are happily serving in their church.

That could be a beautiful example of the outrageous grace of God but for one thing: this couple has become harshly critical of people who are struggling with failures in their lives. When we receive God's grace, let's not forget what kind of people we are. Integrity is missing in situations like this one.

Earlier I was thinking about the kinds of things that could be confessed in totally open relationships. Here is a partial list of privately held imperfections: committing adultery, lusting, indulging in porn, fantasizing sexual relationships and at times masturbating, lying, harboring prejudice, giving in to greed, gossiping and character assassination, drunkenness, drug addictions, abuse of spouse, abuse of children, hypocrisy, vindictive spirits, and unforgiveness, divisiveness that tears apart churches, hatred, arrogance, and ugly pride. You can add to the list if you think of some that would be appropriate to add.

I want to strongly emphasize that what is being discussed in this material is not about sexual sin but about all sin. In the paragraph above we can find failures that are frequently held privately and never confessed. People who hold these sins private are often heartless judges of people who have done what they consider as worse sins.

The purpose of my writing is not to call for a public exposé of all private and unknown sin. The purpose is to call for awareness of the sameness of our situations. We need to be able to admit that there is imperfection in the best of us and gifts from God in the worst of us. Such recognition restrains us from judging harshly others who need the same redeeming grace that we need.

# WHAT MOTIVATES US TO
# AVOID SIN AND DO GOOD?

IF WE ARE redeemed by grace through faith (Ephesians 2:8–9) and not by what we do (works), if there is now no condemnation to those who are in Christ Jesus (Romans 8:1–2), if absolutely nothing can ever separate us from God's love (never ever), then what motivates us or can motivate us to avoid what seems to us to be wrong and lead us to do what seems to us to be right?

There are two basic motivators. People are motivated by a desire for reward (pleasure) and/or fear (pain). Jesus did not forbid rewards. In fact, He spoke often of the rewards people would receive for doing the things that were right. He simply moved rewards from the material world to the spiritual world. He did not promise that people would receive financial reward for service in His kingdom. He did say that they would receive their rewards in heaven and have abundant life (blessedness) in this world. He not only accepted spiritual rewards as a motivation for service, He was not hesitant to use fear of punishment as a deterrent to sin. He warned of separation from God as a result of failure to follow God in this world. To remove all reward and punishment from life is to say that the end of good people is the same as the end of bad people. That implies that we believe that God doesn't care whether we are good or not. That simply cannot be true.

While Jesus gave warnings about the results of failure to follow Him, He consistently urged His followers not to be afraid. Repeatedly in the gospels Jesus urges His disciples to not be afraid. He uses the phrase *fear not*. So while He did warn of things to fear, His major focus was on not being afraid and being motivated by love. The great commandment is to love God with all our hearts and to love our neighbors as we love ourselves.

The apostle Paul follows up on the message of love and not fear. In 2 Timothy 1:7, he says that we are not given a spirit of fear but of love. The Bible in John 4:18 goes further, stating that "perfect love casts out fear and there is no fear in love." So while fear is a motivator, it is certainly not the primary motivator expressed for the followers of Jesus.

In the first eight verses of Matthew 6, the transition is made from improper or wrong motivation to the right motivation for serving in God's Kingdom (Matthew 6:1–8).

## Motivation of Recognition

Practicing piety in order to be recognized by others is doing a good thing for the wrong reason (Matthew 6:1–5). We are to be open in our Christian living, but we are not to be open in order to be recognized for our goodness. In fact, we are to do good in order that God will be recognized through our goodness. Part of the reward that we receive for doing right things is a sense of personal satisfaction. It feels good to do something that we believe in and that we believe is pleasing to God.

We all struggle with our desire to gain recognition and approval from others. That gives people a tremendous power over us. We weigh ourselves down with questions about what they will think or will they like us. Our concern over these issues will influence the stands we take on social, spiritual, and political subjects. I personally struggle with this question: "Am I doing this or saying this because I want the approval of people or am I doing this or saying this because I honestly believe it is right for me?"

Good deeds and right living are to be done inconspicuously. God will reward such goodness in heaven. Again, note and remember that Jesus does not say that good living is rewarded on earth with material things. He does say that reward will be given both in this world and the next. Still, the reward is spiritual in nature. Christians, who still preach the mistaken Old Testament (Mount Sinai) idea that you can measure a person's faithfulness by how they have been blessed with material goods or good health should read carefully this passage. The prosperity gospel that is often promoted by most television preachers is never right and was definitely rejected by Jesus.

In our most optimistic moments we like to think that we would choose good over evil even if we did not believe in God. I am pessimistic about that. I want to believe in the goodness of mankind and I do up to a point. My problem is that I know I am concerned about the self too much, and I suspect others are also. Focusing on what is best for me or even desired by me at this moment often interferes with what is best for others. I confess that I need the constraints and motivations that grow out of my relationship with Jesus Christ. My prayer is that I will more and more be motivated by what is right.

Some still use fear as motivation. Legalistic religious people try to scare people into following their doctrines and lifestyle with the threat of hell. They often add all kinds of physical problems that may result if we do not do what they consider to be right. Fear works for a while but is neither the method used by Jesus nor does it work for long.

Others still use reward to motivate through the promise of prosperity. They tell us that if we do what they instruct us, we will be successful, healthy, and probably rich. That reminds me of the old adage "Early to bed, early to rise and you will be healthy wealthy and wise." An African American friend with whom I worked in Texas said it this way: "Early to bed and early to rise and you will never meet any of the wealthy guys." He was probably closer to the truth than the preachers of the prosperity gospel. Jesus never preached a prosperity gospel, promising to give riches to those who followed him. In fact, he taught just the opposite: following him could lead to poverty and rejection by the world.

So what can motivate us to do what we see as right and avoid what we see as wrong? There are at least three concrete things that can and usually will motivate us to continue to try to please God with our lives after we accept his outrageous grace.

*First, there is gratitude.* I am so thankful for the grace that I have received that there is a desire to thank God for it. I can express my gratitude by trying to serve him in whatever way that I can. That is why I begin every day by giving thanks to God for life and a night's rest. I follow that by asking him to guide my day in his service. Gratitude is a motivator.

*Then there is peace.* When we do what we respect and believe to be right, we generally sense a peace inside us. When we do otherwise, we are usually filled with anxiety and frustration. We begin to question ourselves how could we have done or thought that. Peace returns when we confess and turn back to doing what we believe is right. Peace is a motivator.

*A good feeling.* Akin to peace there is a third thing that can motivate us. It is a deep sense of satisfaction, a good feeling, about what we have done for others and things that we deem to be right for us. I believe Hemingway was right when he said, "I know only that what is moral is what you feel good after and what is immoral is what you feel bad after." Remember times when you have really felt good about something that you have done. I can remember things that have especially made me feel good.

Visiting hospice patients has generated in me good feelings about myself. When I have been privileged to connect with them through conversations and prayer, it is special. I thank God for the opportunity to help comfort them and often to brighten their day.

The chance to share food with needy families is especially satisfying. One of my early memories of such an experience came when I was an adolescent delivering toys and food to poor families in Southeast Missouri.

The memory is of visiting a family with three small children who lived in a rehabbed chicken coop. The floor was dirt, and there was a hole in the metal roof that permitted smoke to escape from the small fire in the middle of the room. That was their heat. I stood in the doorway in disbelief. I thought our family was poor! We gave toys to the children and food for the family. The children brightened with smiles when they received the toys. Seeing them and having a warm feeling and a sense of satisfaction that I seldom experienced was enough to motivate me to seek more good to do.

Another memory is of helping a stray dog when I was in college. The dog was found near our home by a friend who asked me if I would help him pay for a vet to care for the dog. The dog had mange. We took it to a vet and paid a small bill for care, but it seemed like a lot for me. It was more than a day's wages for me, but when we got the dog back in two weeks and let him go in a field near a farmhouse, I felt a sense of satisfaction. The dog running and leaping over a fence was motivation enough for me to seek other ways to help people or animals.

Grace is free and covers all our sin past, present, and future. I have found other, less obvious but practical reasons for avoiding wrong actions and embracing better ones.

On a practical level most of us would agree that we want our families to grow up in safe environments. Those environments are enhanced by people who are striving to do good things and live from what is best in their hearts. Most of us believe that we and our world are better off if we learn to treat each other with respect and integrity. That is a safer world.

Still, on a practical level we probably would agree that a morally upright lifestyle is healthier for us. When we avoid drunkenness, dope addictions, promiscuity, and the like, we more than likely will live longer and with higher-quality lives.

Knowing the practicality of such living in most cases is not a sufficient motivation for living consistently with what we believe to be our best selves. Most of us need more motivation than that.

The recognition that we are loved by God, even before we acknowledge him, can motivate us. The apostle Paul said that the love of Christ controls us (2 Corinthians 5:14). We are held in check by his love.

Maybe a better question is what motivates us to seek God's grace for living? I cannot answer that question for others, but I can tell you that for me, motivation comes from recognizing what a mess we live in. Deep inside I know it can be better, but I can't make it better. I can only trust the grace of God to make it better. That motivates me.

## So What Is the Secret of Motivation for Doing Good?

The real secret for me is that doing good things gives me a reason for living. When I began working as a hospice chaplain, I shared some of my experiences with my eldest son on one of his visits in our home. After a few minutes, he said, "I'm glad you are doing this work. It gives you a reason for getting up in the mornings."

He was right. When I follow what is in my best heart and do good things, I am energized. It is a reason to live. We don't need an audience to cheer us on. We don't need to broadcast our deeds. Passion for living comes from doing deeds of kindness and living from our best heart's urges. In the words of Jesus from Matthew 25, visiting prisoners, feeding the hungry, visiting the lonely, lifting up the fallen (especially when we are unconscious of these deeds) are reasons for entering the kingdom of God.

When I do a survey of my life and remember the things that have meant the most to me, they are the times when I was able to encourage discouraged people, visit sick and lonely people, comfort grieving people, help a couple resolve a conflict, call or write to a lonely person, pick up a stray animal, deliver food to a hungry family, lift an alcoholic or a drug addict up and help them find support, and offer a drink to a thirsty person.

When I worked as a hospice chaplain I started before eight in the morning and often continued until after five or six in the evening. I was given a list of patients to visit in homes, in hospitals, and in care facilities. I made visits to encourage patients, support family members, offer spiritual support to them, and just be with them. I would return to the office to document the activities of the day and then begin to think of the people I would see the next day.

I was privileged to do that work for almost two years. I loved working as a pastor and doing a lot of those things for people in our congregation, but I have never enjoyed work more than when I daily visited critically ill people and tried to help them.

So after all the other reasons listed above, I will simply add that living out of your best heart will give you a passion for life and a reason for living. That is the *why* for serving people even when you know that you are in the circle of God's grace and nothing can separate you from His love.

To the fallen and discouraged reader, I say stand up. You are useful in the kingdom of God. Go find someone who is waiting for your words of encouragement or support. It will give you a passionate reason for living. That is motivation enough! Share God's grace. It is outrageous!

# SIMPLE STEPS TO RECEIVING GOD'S GRACE

IF YOU WANT to receive grace for your failures and acceptance into God's kingdom, there are some simple steps that you can take.

The first step is the recognition and acknowledgement of your spiritual poverty (see the first beatitude in Matthew 5:3). Blessedness is something that we enter in when we receive Jesus into our lives. It is based on poverty of spirit. The literal meaning of poverty of spirit as it is used in this beatitude is to "have no earthly resources at all and thus to put all one's trust in God." When we understand our circumstance, we know that we are utterly helpless before God. We are then to become completely detached from dependence on things. We are to rely on God alone.

The songwriter said it in this way: "Nothing in my hands I bring. Simply to thy cross I cling" (From the third verse of

"Rock of Ages" by Augustus M. Toplady). I have nothing that will commend me to God. I am utterly dependent on God's outrageous grace.

We can have permanent joy, the happiness of God. We can have the blessedness (grace) that Jesus promised in the Beatitudes. How? That question leads us to an even deeper understanding of poverty of spirit. Receiving blessedness (deep, untouchable happiness and grace) begins when we surrender ourselves to Jesus Christ as Lord and Savior. That happens only when we come to Him, acknowledging our spiritual poverty. We are lost and have nothing to commend us to God. We are spiritually bankrupt. The word used by Jesus for poverty in this beatitude is the Greek word *ptochos*. It means "beyond poor." It is absolute abject poverty. William Barclay says that it is a poverty that is beaten to its knees.

Alexander McClaren's description is even more graphic. He says that when Jesus says poor in spirit He is saying, "To be poor in spirit is to be in inmost reality conscious of need, of emptiness, of dependence on God, of demerit; the true estimate of self as blind, evil, weak is intended; the characteristic tone of feeling self-abnegation, like that of the publican smiting his breast." "God have mercy on me, a sinner." Poverty of spirit is what Paul was expressing in Romans when he called himself a wretched man (Romans 7:24).

The absolutely essential point here is that we cannot receive the grace of God unless we are conscious of sin and of our spiritual poverty. Proud confidence seen in personal arrogance must be broken down before we can be useful to God and before we can enter His kingdom. Perhaps the following illustration will make clearer what happens to us when we recognize our poverty stricken condition before God:

I believe that there is similarity between the need to be confronted with our poverty of spirit and what my sons described as their experience in marine corps training. They told me that the corps broke them down and then put them back together as marines. We must somehow be broken of our own self-sufficiency and then put back together as citizens of the kingdom of God.

Most of us tend to resist the truth that is taught here by Jesus. He is saying, "we can only do God's will when we realize our own utter helplessness, our own utter ignorance, our own utter inability to cope with life, and when we put our whole trust in God" (Barclay). This flies in the face of our notions that we can somehow make it in life on our own without any outside help. We are after all independent people, aren't we?

Brokenness, spiritual poverty is a necessary condition for receiving the blessedness of God in our lives. I have been broken by my own awareness of sin, by public humiliation, and failure in my life. In that broken condition, I have fallen on my face before God and pleaded for mercy. It has been when I have had no more resources of my own to pull from that I have finally fallen before God. I had no place else to turn. Those experiences are painful but have led to new awareness of relationship to Jesus. In those times I have learned to celebrate the darkness because I still believe the light of day will again fill my life.

I have a clear memory of the time in my life that I became completely aware of my dependence on Jesus Christ. When I made the decision to admit my helplessness and consciously decided to rely on Him, I became aware of His real living presence. I experienced a new joy and security that I had not known before.

I knew then that I did not need to be afraid to express my faith and take appropriate stands for Christ. I did not need to fear denominational leaders, other authorities, or public opinion. I could now be who I believed God wanted me to be because my source of security was not in myself and not in any externals in this world. I could then understand how the disciples could confront their captors by saying, "Whether it is better to listen to you or to God, you judge. We will obey God." When I slip away from the awareness of my utter dependence on God, I long to find it again. I need His grace every day.

The second step is also simple. It is just asking. When I recognize my own spiritual poverty, I can ask God to give me his grace. He will give it. Jesus said, "Ask and you will receive" (Matthew7:7–8).

I then receive God's grace and mercy. What remains for me is to do the best I can to live in that grace and share that mercy with others. I will not always be able to do that but His grace will still be sufficient for me.

I want to continue asking, accepting, and trusting God for His mercy and grace. I know it sounds outrageous, but that is how the grace of God is.

The third and essential step for us is to be honest with ourselves about our poverty of spirit. We must stop pretending and hiding from one another. We don't need to go around talking about all our sin and failures, but we do need to admit that those things are in our lives and therefore we cannot judge others. We must extend the same grace and mercy to others that we have received.

Of course, underlying all this there is personal faith. Without faith it is impossible to please God.

# THE GIFTS OF GRACE

WE HAVE SEEN that the greatest gift of grace is the forgiveness of our sin and eternal salvation for our souls. I have noted that life itself is a gift of grace, and I know that from firsthand experience. Certainly that is enough, but the outrageous grace of God goes further than that. In His grace God gives us gifts for the struggles of daily living in this world and gifts for service in His kingdom.

Manning notes, "Forgiveness is the key to everything. It forms the mind of Christ in us." The gift of forgiveness is ours when we accept God's grace through faith in Jesus Christ. That redeeming grace brings with it other spiritual gifts.

In general, God's grace gives us the passion and energy to continue living through even difficult circumstances.

My friend Bill is paralyzed from the waist down as a result of back surgery gone wrong. He struggled through depression and anger when he was given the news. He was a robust outdoorsman and now is confined to a wheelchair. After almost a year of struggle, he decided to make the most of his situation. He began to visit people who were in hospitals for surgery or extended illnesses. He visited homes of people who were shut in and became an inspiration to all who knew him. A devout Christian, he is a testimony to the truth that it is not so much what happens to us but the grace in us that enables us to permit positive things to happen even in terrible situations.

Mary, through a series of mistakes, wound up in prison. She had been a devout Christian for all her adult years and a leader among young people before those years. She has found a way to help prisoners deal with educational needs and health needs while serving her time. It amazes me that this frail-looking woman is so strong as to be able to continue her service to others for years of incarceration. God's grace inside her is greater than what has happened to her.

The apostle Paul was imprisoned in Rome. That is what happened to him. What was happening in him was the awareness of God's grace and his personal faith that whatever happened would work for good. He had said so in Romans 8:28. In that same chapter, he had also said that nothing could separate us from the love of God.

Read his letter to the Philippians (written while he was still imprisoned and facing execution). Look at the upbeat message that came through him in that terrible time. He continued to rejoice in his faith regardless of the circumstances because he had the gift of God's grace in him.

What has happened to you? Been divorced? Had personal failure? Had lost a job? The death of someone close to you may have happened. You may have been treated unfairly. People you love may have misunderstood you. There are hundreds of things that may happen to you. So a vital question is this: have you received the gift of God's grace for daily living?

When we go through stressful situations, we lose energy, motivation, enthusiasm, and often health. Recovering may take place in stages or at least it seems that way. For a while, after a tragic experience, a death, a divorce, a failure of our own, or the loss of a job, we survive. We make it through with determination and always by the grace of God. As we go through, we begin to rise to a level above simple survival. We become productive again. Then most are able to rise to the level of transcending the loss, grief, or other stressful situations. Our energy is restored. Motivation returns. Enthusiasm for life and creativity come back, and we feel better.

The process mentioned here may happen quickly for some, while others will find it takes time. I was not aware of how much energy I had lost and how low my creativity level was after a divorce. It was more than a year before my life began to return to normal.

We make it through and begin to really live again after difficult times only if we have the right stuff inside us. The right stuff includes an underlying belief (faith) that we can make it because of the grace of God. Following are some of the specific gifts of God's grace that enable us to survive the struggles of daily living.

## Patience

Knowledge of God's grace gives us the patience to wait. We wait for the maturing of circumstances and the deliverance of God in the midst of our struggles. Jose Marti said, "Strength comes from waiting." James 1:2–4 tells us that when perseverance and patience finish their work in us, we become complete.

We have to learn to wait and let God help us develop strength in us. When we hurry, we may skip right past the very thing that we need to discover.

Waiting is not one of my best things. When I submit a manuscript to a publisher, I am soon saying to my wife, "I wonder when I will hear from them?"

She generally says, "I imagine that it will take more than two days."

This conversation repeats itself too often until there is finally a message from the publisher. If it is positive, I submit a copy for editing and begin the questions again. "I wonder when they will finish the editing." The discipline of delay has been a difficult one for me to learn, but it is a valuable lesson.

In my selfish world I submit my work to a publisher and then fail to focus on the work they are doing for me and for others. It is as if I am saying I expect them to put my work on the front burners and set aside what they are doing for anyone else. That is blatant selfishness. Again, Jesus is right. We must die to ourselves if we are to live for him and for the best. Indeed, a seed must die before it grows.

That same principle applies to all my relationships. I am impatient and unfair to others in my life when I focus only on what makes me feel good, only on what I want. Delay does not make me feel good at first, but I am learning that it can be for the best. Wow! I hardly can believe that I just said that. That has to be God's grace at work!

We sometimes wait for years for the fulfillment of a dream. When the dream is fulfilled, we usually think the waiting was worth it. Some people will read this and become impatient to get to the next point. If that is happening to you, sit back, take a deep breath, and practice the discipline of delay. It is a gift of grace.

## A New Perspective

Problems are overcome, overcome us, or are ignored depending on perspective. Some people practically worship their problems. In a recent, difficult time in my life, I found myself circling my problem at least ten times more than I thought about the presence and power of God in my life. It was as if the problem had me by the throat or mind and would not let go. That was when I read this statement in Briscoe's commentary on Philippians: "Some people worship their problems more regularly and with greater fervor than they worship their Lord." He added that they "generally allow their lives to revolve around them."

That is exactly what I was doing. My perspective needed to change. That had to happen in me. That change began to occur when I consciously began to acknowledge my faith that God could use any problem or situation in my life to bring about good, if I was willing. I was willing. I began to thank God for his grace and power in my life. I confessed that grace was greater than anything I would ever face in my life and certainly greater than what I was facing. That change in perspective made a positive impact on my life.

Helen Keller is one of the people who has been an inspiration to millions of people. I never grow tired of her story. Without sight or hearing because of an illness she suffered at the age of nineteen months, she became an author and lecturer. Her story gives hope to many who struggle with disabilities in life. Read now a powerful quote from her. This is the perspective that was in her:

If I regarded my life from the point of view of the pessimist, I should be undone. I should seek in vain the light that does not visit my eyes and music that does not ring in my ears. I should beg night and day and never be satisfied. I should sit apart in awful solitude, a prey to fear and despair. But since I consider it a duty to myself and others to be happy I escape a misery worse than any physical deprivation.

I cannot read her words without becoming keenly aware of how important it is to maintain a positive perspective in my life.

Of course, there are people who have such negative perspectives that they find a way to deny their reality. Such people seem to think that problems are not a part of real spirituality, so they deny their existence. No matter what is going on in their lives, they tell you that everything is wonderful. They believe that they could not be good people if they have problems in their lives.

Such people would be wise to read the book of Philippians. It gives us an example of some of Paul's struggles. His perspective was that God could use his situation to further the spread of the good news to people in Rome. In Philippians 1:18, Paul said that his problem did not matter. What mattered to him was that Christ was being preached.

There are dozens of scripture passages that help with perspective. Titus 1:15 says, "Unto the pure all things are pure but to those who are corrupted all things are corrupt." Paul is telling Titus that life is all about perspective. In Matthew11, Jesus tells his disciples that it is not outward things that defile life but what comes from inside us. It's what is *in* us that determines the purity or impurity of what is outside. The writer of Proverbs is credited with saying, as a man "thinks within himself, so he is" (Proverbs 23:7). Our thoughts, our perspectives, really control who we are and how we respond to life.

Paul underscores this principle in Philippians 4 when he gives us a list of good things and tells us to think on these things: "Finally, brothers, whatever is true, whatever is honorable, whatever is right, whatever is pure, whatever is lovely, whatever is of good repute, if there is any excellence and if anything worthy of praise, let your mind dwell on these things." (Philippians 4:8). When we develop the habit of positive focus or perspective, life becomes more of what it is intended to be and less of what it has been.

**Hope**

Hope is one of the great gifts of God's grace. Sometimes hope can be outrageous too. I just remember that there is no such thing as false hope—outrageous though it may be, it is still hope.

While I was writing this material, a letter came to me this week from a friend who is serving a twenty-year term in prison. In the course of a struggle and under the influence of alcohol, he accidentally killed a woman. The result was a conviction on manslaughter. He is seventy-five years old and has served eight years of his sentence. I have known him for more than twenty years.

When I visit him, we talk about making the experience as positive as possible, but he understandably struggles with that concept. Reading the book of Philippians from the New Testament is helpful and hopeful for him; Paul wrote that positive book while he was in prison. He has continued to seek ways to do something good with his life.

He has coached sports teams and worked with men who had no high school education. I know that some of them have been helped by him. He struggles, but he keeps on trying.

He is a Christian. I know that he has done wrong, but he is still a recipient of God's grace and love. He was able to maintain a positive attitude for a long time, but the passing of time has eroded that attitude. The more I thought about him, the more I realized that the best thing I could do for him was to try to help him find new hope.

In a recent letter, I sent him a poem I had written about hope. He responded to my letter by writing, "Thank you for the letter and the poem about hope as a rainbow. Truly, hope is about all I have." While it is about all he has, it is a vital thing for him in his difficult circumstance. He is dreadfully sorry for what happened and has to live with the awareness of it every day. He is a man who has a background in strong, religious faith. He definitely believes in the grace of God. Therein is the foundation of his continued hope. Here is the poem I sent to him:

## Hope Is a Rainbow

The symbol of promise is the rainbow
Hope wrapped in brilliant colors that glow
After every storm, the sun comes out,
And shines away our fears and doubt.

After the rain only a gentle mist stays.
Tiny drops are kissed by the sun's rays,
But before the sun can kiss them dry,
They arch in living color across the sky

I may travel to the end of that bow
Until all its colors have lost their glow

There is no pot of gold for me to find
But the promise still fills my mind.

I can face whatever life may bring
For hope enables me to joyfully sing
With a rainbow crossing my sky
I will live with hope until I die.

Though it is a vital part of every life, hope is usually not appreciated until we are aware of a crisis. The sick cling to hope more than the well. The poor need to focus on hope more than the wealthy. Sinners need hope more than saints. Failures grasp for hope more than the successful. The weak reach for hope more than do the strong. Of course, we all need hope and remembering that will help us to cultivate thoughts that reinforce our hope.

The acknowledged sinner hopes for forgiveness. In despair, the sinner looks for hope in passages like 1 John 1:9. There we are promised that when we confess our sins, God forgives us and cleanses us from all unrighteousness. That is what happens as a result of God's grace.

Hope is for a chance to be well again, for the chance to obtain enough to live on, for the forgiveness that all us sinners so desperately need, for the chance to try again, for the strength to make it through each day, for comfort in our grief, and for courage in our times of fear. Remember Paul's statement to the Corinthians: God's grace is sufficient for all things.

Hope grows out of our view of God. Paul calls him the God of hope. He said in Romans 15:13, "May the God of hope fill you with all joy and peace as you trust in him, so that you may overflow with hope by the power of the Holy Spirit." If our God is big enough to handle all these issues and if He loves us as the Bible says that He does, then we can have hope, no matter what our present situation or circumstance.

"How big is our God?" The parent asks the child, "How big are you?"

The child reaches as high over his/her head as possible and says, "This big. God is this big!"

That is important information for us to have and to remember because we will face challenges that require a great deal more strength than we have. Entering a fight when a giant is standing behind you is not as threatening as entering a fight alone. (You are afraid and inadequate until you see the giant!) Whether we see him or not, God, our giant defender, is always standing behind us and beside us. That knowledge changes our perspective and solidifies our hope. It is a gift of God's outrageous grace.

## Perseverance

When bad things happen in my life, my kneejerk reaction is to panic or to begin a path of anxiety-producing thoughts like "This is awful. This is impossible for me to handle." After a time, hours, or even days, I begin to remember the truth. I have made it this far by the grace of God, and that is the beginning of the belief that I can make it further. It takes a little while, but eventually, I am able to push the anxiety-producing thoughts aside with thoughts of faith in God and a belief that his grace and power are available to me and in me.

I am not suggesting an "everything is all right," light-hearted Pollyanna attitude. Often, things are not all right, but they are seldom if ever insurmountable. That is reality. The death of a loved one is an awful experience. The diagnosis of a life-threatening or life-ending disease is awful, but we make it through by continuing to walk and live in the grace of God. I do not believe this is easy, but it must be done, and in God's grace, I will do it.

I was told that my dad was dying. He had suffered a massive stroke. He and I had developed a strong friendship over the years, especially with several trips we made together. There was a lot of talking and a lot of fun. I remembered the first and only time I heard him pray. He agreed to go with me and two other ministerial students to a mission ministry in a nearby jail. On the way, we had a time of prayer, and my dad joined in with a short prayer for all of us on that day. After the stroke, he had trouble communicating at all and was soon totally unable to communicate.

He went into a coma and spent six months in a nursing home. I visited him almost every day. I remember how hard it was to see him lying in bed apparently with no awareness of what was going on around him. Those were difficult days, but they reinforced for me the fact that we can make it through by just putting one foot in front of the other until we reach the end of the struggle.

When I am facing a hard situation now, I just take a deep breath and remind myself that I can make it by the grace of God. I then just put one foot in front of the other and walk through. As an old deacon in the first church I served as a pastor used to tell me, "You just have to keep on keeping on."

Coleman Cox, a motivational writer from the 1920s is credited with the statement, "Even the woodpecker owes his success to the fact that he uses his head and keeps pecking away until he finishes the job he starts." Perseverance means we keep on pecking away until we finish the tasks we begin. Jesus told his disciples that anyone putting his hand to the plow and looking back was not fit for the kingdom of God (Luke 9:62). That kind of perseverance comes only with the grace of God.

## Faith

A man seeking healing for his child was told by Jesus to have faith. The man responded by saying "Lord, I believe. Help my unbelief." Faith is a gift from God. We can't just grit our teeth and try harder to believe. Believing is a gift of Grace.

Faith is belief. All of us have faith. We believe things. We even believe in things. The point for us is to examine what we believe and what we believe in. There are certain faiths I have that enable me to make it through the tough times. I have a faith that the sun will shine somewhere tomorrow and eventually will shine where I am. Even when I walk in darkness, I believe in the sunshine. That helps me.

Here are three practical and helpful illustrations of what inner faith can mean in a crisis:

First, Vern was in the hospital after a severe heart attack. He had already had open-heart surgery and was now in critical condition. I asked him if he thought his condition was life threatening. He said that it was. I asked him if he thought he might die from this condition, and again he responded in the affirmative.

In those circumstances, it was my practice to ask if the patient was afraid. I asked and he said, "No, because I have been trusting Jesus with my whole life. I know I can trust him with my dying." That kind of faith is a gift from God's grace.

The second situation is described in Barbara Davis's own words:

> After the colonoscopy where my cancer was found, I was not allowed to go home because my blood count was so low. I had to be admitted and given a blood transfusion. I lay in the hospital bed crying and feeling sorry for myself. I was sure I was going to die. All of a sudden a voice came into my head that said, "Barbara, haven't I always been with you? I am with you always. I will get you through this just trust me and lean on me."
>
> When I asked if I could go home for a day or two, the surgeon said, "You are a very sick woman. You may go home on one condition. I want you to pray and I will pray for a good outcome." I agreed and went home for two days. When they wheeled me into surgery, he asked if I had prayed. I told him that I had and whatever happened was okay because God was with me. When he came out to see my family, he said he had never seen a more successful outcome with such a serious surgery. God had to remind me to have faith. I am so grateful for His love.

The third example is from the experience and writing of Senator Jean Carnahan. After several tragedies in her life including the loss of her husband and a son in a plane crash and the loss of most of her personal belongings and country home in a fire, she writes that she was alone in her home when the electric power went out, leaving her in the darkness. After calling the electric company and being assured that it was being taken care of, she was able to peacefully go to sleep to awake to restored power in the morning.

She observes that her ability to sleep was the assurance that the problem was being handled. She then adds about her faith in God that "whether we know it or not He is behind the scenes working on our problems and seeking to restore our lives. In the darkest hours of our lives, His promises are ours: 'Don't be afraid. I've got your hand. We're in this together.'" That is the kind of faith that enables us to walk through the darkness.

We should be preparing ourselves for the crisis that will come to all of us. We do that by exercising our faith through prayer as we ask God to help our unbelief through the gift of his wonderful, outrageous grace.

## Peace

I have recently learned things that I wish I had known fifty years ago. I believe this lesson is a gift of God's grace. Here is an attempt to sum up a powerful concept. Acts of selfishness cannot produce peace. We are meant to be better than that. Peace comes when we bring together our best desires with our outward actions.

That concept will be clearer and more helpful with an illustration. I drove by a nursing home on my way to a casino. I knew a man who was in that nursing home, and I knew that he would be helped by a visit. My best desire and best self knew that it would be a good thing for me to stop and visit with him. Besides, I have been saying for months that I should never go back into a casino. What happens in my heart if I pass by and proceed to the casino without stopping to see this man who is definitely in need? What happens is that there is no congruence between my best self and my actions? That can never produce a heart of peace.

What happens in me if I pull into the parking lot of the nursing home and spend the next hour visiting with this needy man? I will feel harmony inside. That is the music made by blending my best internal awareness with my real outward action. That creates a heart of peace in me and will produce calmness and joy in my emotions. This enables me to do more creative things with my day. I am immediately more patient with people and feel comfortable relating to them.

There are dozens of illustrations of how we can develop a heart of peace within. For instance, when I see a home-less man on the street and believe I can encourage him, I become aware of a helpful urge in my heart. If I act on that urge and help the man, I let peace happen in my heart. If I ignore the best urges, I cause conflict to happen in my heart.

For me, the search for inner peace is a constant challenge. Getting into an atmosphere that is conducive to inner calm helps me. I can close my eyes in such an atmosphere and take a few deep breaths to relax my muscles. But I still have to find a way to deal with the kind of thoughts that started this day for me.

All of our struggles to find peace can come to fulfillment if we are able to accept the peace that is promised through Jesus Christ. He said, "Peace I leave with you, my peace I give you" (John 14:27).

William Barclay points out that peace is not absence of trouble. Peace, he says, is everything that makes for our highest good. "The peace which Jesus offers us is the peace of conquest. It is the peace which no experience in life can ever take from us. It is the peace which no sorrow, no danger, no suffering can make less. It is the peace which is independent of outward circumstances" (Barclay's commentary on John's Gospel).

The peace described here is a peace for which I pray often. It is a gift from God that is available to us but too seldom experienced. God, please put this peace in us.

Consistent peace of God within enables us to face the crisis in life without panic. We are able to walk through whatever comes with a calm assurance that when all is said and done, everything will be all right. That is outrageous grace in action.

## Security

When I use the word *security*, I mean "personal internal security." Security is an elusive goal for most of us. So little gives us lasting personal security. Riches cannot do it. Power or position cannot do it. Nothing that can be taken from us can give us a sense of security.

A sense of security, like peace, is something that happens in us as a result of God's grace. For me, that sense of security needs to be grounded deep, deep within because so many things threaten us every day. I want and pray for a sense of security that cannot be shaken by threats, temptations, failures, illness, or any other external events including death. This means that it must be based on something that is indestructible.

We need a sense of that personal security to enable us to face the challenges of life. When I was going through the fear of facing my responsibility in dealing with racial prejudice, I had only one source of personal security that meant anything to me. It was that my security rested entirely in my relationship with God. I believed in Jesus Christ and accepted him by faith through grace not only as Savior and Lord but also as my ultimate security.

At one point in my life I became keenly aware of the presence of God. It was so real that I thought I could reach out and touch Him. Once I realized that God was really near and in me, I was free to take the stands that I needed to take. My only regrets in life have been when I failed to do what I believed was right even to the point of seeking security and personal acceptance outside of faith.

While the ultimate security comes to us through our faith, some personal security comes from the families that nurtured us as we grew up. We are more likely to sense security if we have lived in a home where love was expressed regularly and abundantly. It is difficult to feel secure if we grew up in a negative atmosphere of conflict and criticism. Parents are well served if they become conscious of these facts when their children are young and still living in the home. If we encourage and express love to our children, we are building security in them and creating a heart of peace in ourselves. Since we do not choose our parents, even families are a gift of grace.

## Gratitude

"A thankful heart is the parent of all virtues" (Cicero). In all this material, I am suggesting that we have been given traits and gifts that are able to help us handle whatever happens to us. These are gifts; therefore, they deserve an expression of our gratitude to the giver. We would not be able to make it through many things in life without the grace and mercy that bring us the characteristics in us that empower us. To experience all these things or even have the opportunity to experience them calls for a thankful heart.

We don't always think of gratitude as being a power. It is certainly an attitude and an action that we all know we need. It is not a stretch to recognize thanksgiving as a powerful action. Giving thanks is a part of worship. As said in the Bible, "Come, let us sing for joy to the Lord; Let us shout joyfully to the rock of our salvation. Let us come before His presence with thanksgiving. Let us shout joyfully to Him with psalms." (Psalms 95:1–2).

All the gifts that we need come from God. The major gift is the gift of Jesus for life and guidance. That is why Paul wrote, "Thanks be to God for his indescribable gift" (2 Corinthians 9:15). We are ill equipped to use the gifts we have received unless we have a grateful heart within us.

Our circumstances are not changed by our gratitude but our perspective of them is transformed by expressions of thanksgiving. It is said in the Bible, "in everything give thanks; for this is God's will for you in Christ Jesus" (1 Thessalonians 5:18).

We are promised that we are a part of Gods eternal kingdom. That is why Paul could say with assurance that nothing separates us from God's love. Again the Bible says,

"Therefore since we are receiving a kingdom that cannot be shaken, let us show gratitude, by which we may offer to God an acceptable service with reverence and awe;" (Hebrews 12:28).

Ultimate victory is ours as said in the Bible: "Thanks be to God. He gives us victory through our Lord Jesus Christ" (1 Corinthians 15:57).

When we give thanks, we feel better about ourselves. Gratitude is an expression from our best desires. Those best desires, when fulfilled, bring about higher levels of energy and passion for living that empowers us to make it through whatever has come into our lives.

I am learning, not only to give thanks for what has been but for what is going to be. I know that it is right for me to thank God for his promises to me even before they become reality. For me, having a grateful heart for God's provisions, past and future, is a tremendously powerful way to transform whatever is going to happen to me.

When thanksgiving becomes a conscious part of our hearts, we have a wonderful tool for redeeming our future. When I begin to become concerned about what may happen to me in the future, I remind myself to immediately give thanks to God for the fact that he is already taking care of the future. His redeeming grace reaches into the past (forgiveness), the present (strength for living), and the future (caring for our problems even before they occur.)

When I remember all this, my prayers become my praise to God for his grace and love. That is part of my worship.

I pray that God will equip us with all the things that we need in us to face whatever happens to us. I also pray that he will give us the wisdom to express gratitude for them all, even before we experience them.

These are only a few of the gifts of God's grace but perhaps enough for us to build on.

# THE MOST AMAZING THING
## ABOUT GOD'S GRACE

I LOVE WRITING and especially writing about God's grace. I enjoy writing and generally fall in love with a manuscript while I am writing it. I love this manuscript so much that I don't want to leave it. For me, it is important to leave it with a strong finish. This is it for me. This is the most amazing thing about a grace that I call outrageous.

Other than lifting us out of our lost condition, forgiving us of sin, and giving us eternal life, grace gives us special gifts for living. I have listed several of them in the preceding chapter. I close with a focus on one of those gifts. It requires some explanation. To explain it, I refer first to Paul's letter to the Colossians.

Paul prayed for the Colossians that they would be able to live lives that please God in every way and produce good work as they grew in the knowledge of God (Colossians 1:10–14) Then he gave us this remarkable passage: "Being strengthened according to his glorious might so that you may have great endurance and patience, and joy." He adds that God has redeemed us and given us dominion over darkness and brought us into the kingdom of the Son He loves. His Son has brought us forgiveness of sin.

This is a powerful passage and has come to have a very special meaning to me. Note the words *great endurance*, *patience*, and *joy*. A few years ago I was reading William Barclay's commentary on the book of James. He pointed out that the same word translated *great endurance* in Colossians can be translated "unswerving constancy." It is a strange-sounding Greek word. Literally, the word in Greek is *hupomone* (hoop-o-mon-e).

In the book of James, the word is translated "patience." It is that patience that is a most amazing gift for me. But the word *patience* is totally inadequate to convey the depth of that word and the meaning it can have for us. The word means the quality not only to suffer things but also to welcome them and vanquish them. It is what enabled the Christian martyrs to die singing songs of faith. It is a composite of a lot of the things included in this book as things that enable us to face the difficulties of life without giving up.

Barclay sums up the meaning of the word as not only the "ability to bear things but the ability in bearing them to turn them into glory. It is a conquering patience. *Hupomone* is the ability to deal triumphantly with anything that life can do to us."

More than any other thing that I know other than grace itself, I would rather be given the gift of hupomone. The presence of that powerful gift from God brings with it peace, joy, courage, security, patience, hope, perseverance, positive perspective, and knowledge of the way to live. The very thought of it brings encouragement to me.

This is a gift that is strengthened with use. The more we face the tests of life with this great endurance, unswerving constancy of spirit, the stronger we become to face the next test. None of us want to suffer, but we recognize that often our suffering is an opportunity to demonstrate to the world the endurance and constancy of spirit that comes from the indwelling presence of God in our lives. With this power in us, it really matters little what happens to us because God's grace will show us through.

One size fits all. The same grace that brought salvation into our lives brings the power to face the greatest difficulty as well as the nagging problems of daily living. A wonderful thing about this gift is that we don't have to wait for a dramatic crisis to experience it. As the power of a great dynamo can be used to generate the capacity to move tremendous equipment, it can also be used to illumine a small nightlight in my bedroom. The same majestic power of God that enabled martyrs to die singing praises can also enable us to deal with the everyday issues of life. Don't be reluctant to exercise this gift to help overcome a tiny obstacle. We will never use up the power of God.

That is the reason I am not reluctant to pray for God's help in everything. Nothing is too small (not even a sparrow falling to earth) and nothing is too great to go beyond his concern and power. The practicality of Christianity is that it is not only to give us hope for eternity but hope for overcoming the impatience that we experience when we wash dishes.

The older I grow, the more I have learned to talk with God about everything in my life. I used to spend a lot of time talking to myself (my wife says I still do), but now I replace much of that with talking to God. When I walk down stairs, I may say, "Lord, what am I doing down here? Am I looking for something?" When I remember the answers, I say, "Thank you, God." I am dead serious when I tell you that I am learning to talk to God about everything.

My youngest daughter has a master's degree in business. She recently applied for a job as an aide in a school near her home. She first told, "You are overqualified for this job."

She said, "I don't care. I just want to work with children in this school."

God does not seem to consider himself overqualified to deal with our everyday issues. He just wants to be with us and help us with our daily needs. I guess if we can't trust him with the small things, we will have more trouble trusting him with the major ones.

It is an overwhelming thought to realize that we have in us a power that is sufficient to create worlds and it is available to us to confront daily life. Wow!

So we can take hope no matter what our circumstance. If we have fallen, we can stand. If we have failed, we can be forgiven. If we are fearful, we can have courage. If we are dying, grace will be provided as needed. We are without excuse because we have with us the outrageous grace of God for living. We can victoriously make it through anything in life.

When we clearly understand that what happens to us is not as important as what is in us, we are able to work through anything. It is then that we begin to understand that when we trust in God's grace, what happens to us really happens for us. All of life can work together for good (Romans 8:28).

# CONCLUSION

IT IS ALL about grace. That is the theme of this book. One of the conclusions is that we all need grace every day of our lives and the good news is that God provides that grace abundantly, or in keeping with the theme of this book, outrageously.

When we have taken the steps outlined above and entered into a life of grace, we have an opportunity to live out that grace. Think about what that means.

These are a couple of very important themes to remember:

Remember that good and evil live in us alongside each other. Some days we live in the kingdom of God where there is love, peace, joy, faith, courage, purity, grace, and mercy. On other days we slip out of the kingdom and live unholy lives. This is why we will always need grace in our lives.

I am not writing about theology. I don't care if your theology says that "once in the kingdom of God, always in the kingdom of God" because that is an ideal that is never realized, and because it is promoted as truth, it becomes a source of discouragement to many. Better stated, "Once in the circle of God's grace and love, we never fall outside that circle." The fact is that, not theologically but on a practical level, we are in and out of the kingdom of God repeatedly.

Remember that peace can guide us and keep us living out the best in us. Perhaps the concept becomes clearer when we think of the choices we make. In the book *The Anatomy of Peace*, there is the clear statement that we have in us either a heart of peace or a heart of war. That is the wording used to describe the peaceful heart versus the troubled heart. When we follow the best desires of our hearts, we are filled with peace, but when we deny the best desires and follow other desires, we are filled with trouble and conflict. We can move from one heart to the other in a second by the choices we make.

It is stated above that peace is one of the things that motivates us to continue living a life of service to God. Becoming aware of peace in our hearts is vital to living out of a life of grace. We can learn to live out of a heart of peace.

When I choose to love and act in love toward others, my heart is at peace. When I fail to act in love toward others and become selfish, my heart is at war within me. I cannot help others except from a heart of peace. When I am at war within myself, I cannot help others find peace, and I cannot coexist with them in peace.

Hearts of peace permit a river of love and healing to flow from us (John 7:38). I have never fully understood this concept, but I know that there are people who seem to give off positive feelings when we are around them. When such a person walks into a room, people begin to feel better. People like that are people who have hearts of peace.

Hearts of war cause troubled waters of tension, anxiety, and aggression to flow from us. Jesus taught his disciples to "let not your hearts be troubled. Believe in God. Believe in Me" (John 14:1). Troubled hearts certainly are inconsistent with productive living and right living.

The psalmist prayed for a clean heart to be created in him because only then could he experience the joy of his faith in God and be able to teach others the ways of the Lord (Psalm 51:10).

Jesus taught that out of good hearts there flow works of righteousness but out of evil hearts flow evil works (Matthew 12:34–35). The fact is that we cannot produce healthy relationships if there is not a positive flow from our hearts. First, settle into your own heart. Cleanse it by the renewing of your mind daily. Fill your mind with thoughts of love, peace, grace, joy, kindness, and all the fruits of the spirit (Galatians 5:22). Then, with a heart filled with peace, you can be a positive influence on the people around you.

Matthew 7:6 and Isaiah 24:13 indicate that there must be harmony between our hearts and our words. If our words and deeds are producing conflict, we have a heart problem. If our hearts are healed and filled with peace, we have healthy hearts. We are seeking what is called *congruence*. The primary purpose of prayer is to bring our lives (hearts) into harmony with the teachings of Jesus. When we do that, we are becoming congruent. There is power in congruent living.

Our world can never be at peace, our relationships will never be at peace, and our own lives will never be filled with peace until we begin to live out of our best hearts, the hearts of peace.

What brings peace? Peace comes from expressing gratitude. The apostle Paul wrote to the Philippians that they should "not be anxious about anything, but in everything, by prayer and petition, with thanksgiving, present your requests to God. And the peace of God, which transcends all understanding will guard your hearts and your minds in Christ Jesus" (Philippians 4:6–7)

Years ago, Rolland Brown told me that he believed peace flows from a faucet that we cannot reach. He said that we can reach the faucet that turns on thanksgiving and a hand that we cannot see turns on peace. Peace comes from gratitude.

Love (loving others as we love ourselves) also brings peace into our hearts and lives. Think of a person that you love as much as you love anyone else in the world. What do you feel when you think of that person? Most of us can think of children that we love. We think of a spouse that we love. We think of a parent or grandparent. You may even think of a special friend that you love. Thoughts of those people warm our hearts and give us a deep sense of peace.

Unselfish behaviors and words will bring peace. When we do something really helpful for others, we generally get a good feeling from it. One of my friends was with his wife at a nice restaurant in Kansas City. They noticed a young couple that appeared to be celebrating, perhaps their prom night. They studied the menu nervously, and at one point, the young man checked his wallet. My friend called the waiter over and told him to tell the young couple that they should order whatever they wanted that their bill would be paid for them. He requested that the waiter not reveal the donor. He told me that he really felt joy as the couple looked around the room to see if they recognized anyone. That kind of feeling translates into peace. The more unselfishly that we live and the more we follow our best desires, the more peace we have internally.

Alleviating suffering is a characteristic of those who live in the kingdom of God. I have never felt better than when I was privileged to help alleviate the fear of a cancer patient who thought he was dying within a month. A year later, we celebrated together. My wife and I had that repeated experience several times over the ten years that we operated the

Cancer Support Center of St. Louis. When we are engaged in helping to ease the pain of anyone who is suffering, we are filled with the awareness of God's peace. We are presently continuing to experience peace in our hearts as we work with hospice patients.

Prayer is an essential part of living in the Spirit and in the kingdom of God. It is the activity best ascribed as seeking to bring our lives into harmony with the will and love of God. That is certainly a way to a peaceful heart.

When we are defensive, when we are behaving in selfish ways, when we are argumentative, when we are worrying, we are living in a troubled heart.

When we are resolving problems, when we are helping others, when we are contented with life, we are living in a heart of peace. We simply cannot be a positive influence unless we are living in a heart of peace. This heart is found in the grace that is the kingdom of God.

A general conclusion is that when we accept the grace of God into our lives, we will want to live in a manner that is consistent with the teachings of Jesus Christ, specifically the teachings of the Sermon on the Mount. The following is a brief summary of those teachings:

- *Priorities and making kingdom investments.* Jesus is not speaking here of being unwise in planning for the future. He is pointing out the wrong priority. Our focus is to be in the kingdom of God (Matthew 6:19).

- *The right priority.* This is to lay up treasure in heaven and seek the kingdom of God above all else. Few people ever really do this (Matthew 6:20–21).
- *We must choose.* We choose to lay up treasure in heaven not like the man who had two calves and in gratitude gave one of them to God. When one calf died, he said, "God's calf died!" That is not the kind of choosing Jesus is talking about. Everything we have belongs to him (Matthew 6:24).
- *Obedience is vital.* The teachings of Jesus always assume obedience. The way to get close to God is through obedience because obedience is an indication of love. Jesus asks us all the same question He asked Simon Peter: "Do you love Me?" If the answer is yes, then we are to obey by doing His will, and that may even involve feeding His sheep. Not church attendance, not the religious things you and I do, but loving obedience is the key to knowing God. It begins with faith in Jesus and His grace. That is followed by obedience to His teachings. The more we obey, the more we know.
- *Trust is the end of worry.* Accepting Christ's authority puts an end to worry. All we have to do is obey Him.

He will take care of us. Jesus uses nature to illustrate His point.

The Sermon on the Mount by Jesus places the highest demands possible on those of us who would follow Him. When I read back over this book, I know it is humanly impossible to live up to these teachings. We absolutely must rely on the grace and mercy of God. Put God first and trust Him. Accept His outrageous grace.

# BIBLIOGRAPHY

Barclay, William. *The Letter to the Romans*. Philadelphia: The Westminster Press, 1957.

Covey, Stephen R. *The 7 Habits of Highly Effective People*. New York: Simon and Schuster, 1989.

Lakoff, George. *Moral Politics: How Liberals and Conservatives Think*. University of Chicago Press, 1996.

Lucado, Max. *In the Grip of Grace*. Dallas, Texas: Word Publishing, 1996.

Maclaren, Alexander. *Expositions of Holy Scripture*. Grand Rapids, Michigan: Eerdmans, 1932.

Manning, Brennan. *All Is Grace*. David C. Cook, 2011.

Manning, Brennan. *The Signature of Jesus: The Call to a Life Marked by Holy Passion and Relentless Faith*. Rev. ed. Sisters, Oregon: Multnomah Publishers, 1996.

Swindoll, Charles R. The Grace Awakening. Dallas, Texas: Word Publishing, 1990.

The Arbinger Institute. *The Anatomy of Peace: Resolving the Heart of Conflict.* San Francisco, California: Berrett-Koehler, 2006.

Made in the USA
Lexington, KY
26 January 2017